A Concise
Catholic
Catechism

Tony + Mary,

MODELS OF FAITH!

KEEP IT!
ENJOY IT!
SPREAD IT!

Love

Mike

A Concise Catholic Catechism

EDITED BY
MICHAEL SHAUGHNESSY

BURNS & OATES
A Continuum imprint
LONDON • NEW YORK

Burns & Oates

The Tower Building   370 Lexington Avenue

11 York Road   New York NY 10017-6503

London SE1 7NX

www.continuumbooks.com

First published 2002

British Library Cataloguing-in-Publication Data
A catalogue record for this book is available from the British
Library.

ISBN 0-8264-6571-4

Typeset by YHT Ltd, London
Printed and bound by Bath Press, Bath

Nihil obstat: Father Anton Cowan
Censor
Imprimatur: Monsignor Tom Egan V.G.
Westminster, 14 April 2001

The Nihil obstat *and* Imprimatur *are a declaration that a book or pamphlet is considered to be free from doctrinal or moral error. It is not implied that those who have granted the* Nihil obstat *and* Imprimatur *agree with the contents, opinions or statements expressed.*

Contents

Each paragraph in *A Concise Catholic Catechism* is numbered. This number also corresponds to its endnote.

The Creed

I believe in God the Father

I believe in Jesus Christ, the only Son of God

He was conceived by the Holy Spirit and born of the Virgin Mary

Jesus Christ suffered under Pontius Pilate was crucified, died and was buried

He descended into hell and on the third day he rose again

I believe in the Holy Catholic Church

I believe in the forgiveness of sins

I believe in the resurrection of the body

I believe in life everlasting

Part Two:
The Sacraments

The Liturgy

The Sacraments of Christian Initiation

The Sacrament of Baptism

The Sacrament of Confirmation

The Sacrament of the Eucharist

The Sacraments of Healing

The Sacrament of Reconciliation

The Sacrament of the Anointing of the Sick

The Sacraments at the Service of Communion and Mission

The Sacrament of Holy Orders

The Sacrament of Matrimony

Other Liturgical Celebrations

Part Three:
The Ten Commandments

Our Vocation

The Ten Commandments

The First Commandment

The Sixth Commandment

The Eighth Commandment

The Ninth Commandment

The Tenth Commandment

Part Four:
Prayer

Christian Prayer

The Lord's Prayer

Foreword

Without any question, one of the most important Catholic publications of the last half-century has been the *Catechism of the Catholic Church*. Within it is contained the distillation and the synthesis of the thought of the Second Vatican Council. The catechism went through several drafts and was the fruit of extensive consultation – every Bishops' Conference throughout the world was consulted on each draft. It is an authoritative presentation of the mind and teaching of the Catholic Church today and should be the basis of every future catechism and every catechetical programme in today's Church.

For this to be accomplished there must be a growing familiarity with the *Catechism of the Catholic Church* – and this on two levels – the level of the theologian and expert catechist and the level of the parish catechist, teacher and ordinary reader. It is on this second level that *A Concise Catholic Catechism* will prove extremely useful. It provides an admirable summary of the *Catechism of the Catholic Church* but has reduced the total number of paragraphs from 2685 to 450. It does not go into theological nuances or great detail, but provides a succinct outline of Catholic belief. The serious reader or enquirer will then be drawn to the longer Catechism, which is handily cross-referenced in the appendix to this volume.

The author, Michael Shaughnessy, has served as an Ecumenical Officer in the Diocese of Westminster for the past five years. He is a member of an ecumenical religious order, the Servants of the Word, which was started in Ann Arbor, Michigan, in 1971 with the blessing of the Catholic Bishop. Members of this world-wide community make lifelong commitments to the evangelical counsels of poverty, chastity and obedience. It now includes many Christian traditions in its membership and sponsors related, lay ecumenical communities. Michael is to be thanked and congratulated upon the production

of this helpful summary of Catholic belief
and practice.

The Right Reverend James O'Brien
Chairman of the Westminster Diocesan
Ecumenical Commission

Preface

The search for truth is ultimately a search for God. It is a lifelong task that will remain uncompleted for us all. The fullness of truth is simply beyond our finite minds. Many of us were taught some of the basic truths as children in catechism classes. What was adequate then for a child's faith is inadequate now for an adult's faith. Christians need resources for strengthening their faith. It is for these men and women that this catechism has been written.

Many Catholics find a new eagerness to know what the Christian faith is all about when they come into an experience of the living God through an Alpha Course, a Life in the Spirit Seminar, a prayer group, a bible study or some other means of encounter with the Lord. This awakens a new hunger to grow deeper in their understanding of God and his truth. It is for these men and women that this catechism has been written.

Many non-Catholics have heard something of the Catholic faith and want to know more, quickly and simply. They rightly think they might find something in the *Catechism of the Catholic Church*, but are put off by its length. It is for these men and women that this catechism has been written.

A Concise Catholic Catechism summarizes in 450 paragraphs the key doctrines contained in the 2685 paragraphs of the *Catechism of the Catholic Church*. This means it is possible to read in one sitting.

A Concise Catholic Catechism is based solely on the *Catechism of the Catholic Church*. Over 80 per cent of *A Concise Catholic Catechism* comes directly from the *Catechism of the Catholic Church*. Where *A Concise Catholic Catechism* differs is in wording changed to be more 'user friendly'. So, for example, some of the more technical theological terms used in the *Catechism of the Catholic Church* have been replaced with simpler ones.

There is no teaching or doctrine in *A Concise Catholic Catechism* that cannot be found in the *Catechism of the Catholic Church*. It also follows the order and structure of the *Catechism of the Catholic Church* and every paragraph is cross-referred in the notes to the *Catechism of the Catholic Church.**

By its very nature *A Concise Catholic Catechism* is not light reading. Some paragraphs must be read very carefully in order to comprehend what is in them. Paragraph three for example: 'There are convincing arguments that show God exists. Simplified, they show that God is the first mover, that he is the source of the world's order and beauty, that the infinite exists and that our interior experience leads us to believe.' To comprehend what is said in these forty-one words takes some effort.

A Concise Catholic Catechism is not written to explain or to justify the doctrine of the Church, rather simply to state it. Thus, nothing more is said about why 'our interior experience leads us to believe', or on why this is a reasonable argument for the existence of God. Generally, if you want the doctrine explained or justified, you will need to access other theological writing.

In addition, faith is a mystery. That does not mean *we cannot understand what we*

---

*Because of the IN BRIEF sections of the *Catechism of the Catholic Church* there are times when *A Concise Catholic Catechism* appears not to follow the same order.

believe, rather that certain elements of the faith are beyond our ability to understand *fully*. This is especially true of the great mysteries of faith: the Trinity, the Incarnation, Redemption, and the mystery of good and evil.

The translators of the *Catechism of the Catholic Church* struggled with the question of how far to go in using inclusive language. In the end they decided to stick with the term 'man' rather than 'humanity', 'humankind', 'person' or 'human being'. In *A Concise Catholic Catechism* the same issue had to be faced. You will find that *A Concise Catholic Catechism* uses more inclusive language simply because it is generally written in the first person plural rather than the third person singular, thus 'man's obligations' becomes 'our obligations'.

There are certain contexts where 'man' is indispensable and in these contexts it has been retained. If 'humanity', 'human beings', or 'the human race' adequately convey the meaning of the doctrine, they are used instead.

I trust you will find the truth of the faith summarized here to be inspiring but succinct.

Michael Shaughnessy S.W.

Part One

The Profession of Faith

Introduction

1 **God created us to be happy with him for ever**

God created us to be happy with him for ever, in his own state of blessedness: paradise. Therefore he gave us a desire that draws us to himself, to know him and love him. Only in him will we find the truth and happiness we are searching for.

2 **God calls us to himself**

God calls us to himself so we can find true life and happiness. We cannot find God without his help, but we also need the help of others, in addition to our own efforts.

3 **We can know God**

There are convincing arguments that show God exists. Simplified, they show that God is the first mover, that he is the source of the world's order and beauty, that the infinite exists and that our interior experience leads us to believe.

4 We can resist knowing God

Although it is possible for us to attain a true and certain knowledge of God, we are hampered by the distractions of our senses, imagination and appetites, which are disordered as a consequence of original sin. Yet, even if we forget God or reject him, God continues to call us to himself.

5 God is beyond definition

Since we are limited to human ways of knowing and thinking, our knowledge of God is also limited and our language about him is equally so. Our human words always fall short of the mystery of God.

6 God reveals himself to us

Through divine revelation God makes himself known *directly* to us just as he revealed himself directly to people like Adam, Noah, Abraham, Isaac, Jacob, Moses, David and the prophets in the Old Testament. As with them he has offered us to be in a covenant relationship with him.

7 The full revelation of God is in Jesus

In Jesus Christ the Father has revealed himself fully. He has said everything; there will be no other word than this one. Christ, the Son of God made man, is the Father's one, perfect and unsurpassable Word.

8 The revelation is handed on

In order that the full Gospel might always be preserved in the Church, the apostles, in their preaching and writing, handed on what Christ told them. They appointed bishops as their successors and gave them their own apostolic position of teaching authority.

9 Tradition

What the apostles handed on from Jesus to their successors is called Tradition. Tradition also refers to the continued living transmission of the truth in the Church still going on today. *Tradition* is especially concerned with the doctrine, life and worship of the Church and is something distinct from the *traditions* of the Church.

10 The Magisterium

The Magisterium; that is, the bishops in communion with the successor of Peter; is the living teaching office of the Church. To it alone belongs the task of giving an authentic interpretation of Tradition and Scripture. Even so, the Magisterium is not superior to Scripture and Tradition but is their servant.

11 God's revelation is one

God's revelation is one. Sacred Tradition and Sacred Scripture make up a single sacred deposit: the Word of God. Scripture is also one. Christians read the Old Testament in the light of Jesus Christ risen from the dead. The New Testament is hidden in the Old and the Old Testament is unveiled in the New.

12 God reveals himself in Sacred Scripture

God has revealed himself through Sacred Scripture. He is its author and he inspired its human authors to write his saving truth which firmly, faithfully, and without error teaches that which, for the sake of our salvation, God wished to see confided to the Sacred Scriptures.

13 Interpreting Scripture

To interpret Scripture correctly we must be

attentive to what the human authors intended, the conditions of time and culture, the
literary forms used, and the modes of feeling,
speaking and narrating then current. Sacred
Scripture also must be read and interpreted
in the light of the Holy Spirit by whom it
was written.

14 The books of the Bible

The Church decided which books to include
in the Bible. She included the seventy-three
books that had been used in the Tradition of
the Church. Forty-six are in the Old Testament and twenty-seven in the New Testament, but all Sacred Scripture is one book,
and this one book is Christ.

The Creed

15 Belief in the Creed

Very early the Church recognized the need
for a common confession of faith that would
be standard for all. She expressed and handed on her faith in brief formulae such as the
Apostles' Creed. The Apostles' Creed is so
named because it is a faithful summary of the
apostles' faith.

16 I believe

Faith is a supernatural gift from God. It joins the whole person to God and involves an assent of the intellect and will. 'I believe' has thus a twofold reference: to the person, and to the truth. To obey in faith is to submit to God and to his word.

17 Models of faith

Abraham is offered to us by Sacred Scripture as the model of the obedience of faith. The Virgin Mary is its most perfect embodiment. She both believed and obeyed. 'Behold I am the handmaid of the Lord; let it be done to me according to your word.'

18 Faith is trust

Believing in God befits the dignity of the human person because it is a free and conscious act. Faith is entrusting oneself wholly to God and believing absolutely in what he says. Faith can be more certain than all human knowledge because it is founded on the very word of God, who cannot lie.

19 Faith is necessary for salvation

Faith is a gift from God that we cannot even receive without the help of the Holy Spirit. Without faith it is impossible to please God; without faith no one has ever endured to the end, and attained justification and eternal life; without faith in Jesus Christ we cannot be saved.

20 Our faith will be tested

Faith is often put to the test by experiences of evil, suffering, injustice and death. Such tests can tempt us to reject our faith. Therefore we must fight the good fight, and persevere in faith until the end of our lives.

21 The Church's faith

The Church's faith precedes, brings about, supports, and nourishes our faith. The Church is therefore called the mother of all believers. No one can have God as Father who does not have the Church as Mother.

22 We believe in the one true God

We firmly believe and confess without reservation that there is only one true God, eternal, infinite, unchangeable, unfathomable, almighty and indescribable.

23 God's unique existence

God's name is mysterious just as God is a mystery. His name, YHWH ('I AM WHO AM') means that God alone IS. God is without beginning or end. He does not receive his existence from anything else, and anything else that is receives its existence from him.

24 Respecting God's holy name

Out of respect for the holiness of God, the people of Israel do not pronounce his name. The revealed name (YHWH) is replaced by the divine title 'LORD' (in Hebrew *Adonai*, in Greek *Kyrios*). By using this title we acclaim the divinity of Christ saying: 'Jesus is LORD'.

25 God is truth and love

God is the source of truth because he made heaven and earth and knows them perfectly. God is the source of love because he himself is an eternal exchange of love – Father, Son and Holy Spirit – and he has destined us to share in that love.

26 The Triune God

The mystery of the Trinity is the central mystery of Christian faith because it is the mystery of God in himself. It is the source of all the other mysteries of faith and the light that enlightens them, because all God does comes out of who he is as Father, Son and Holy Spirit. It is the most important and essential teaching in the 'hierarchy of the truths of faith'.

27 One God in three persons
We worship one God in the Trinity and the Trinity in unity, without either confusing the persons or dividing the substance; for the Father's person is one, the Son's is another, the Holy Spirit's another; but the Godhead, the Father, Son and Holy Spirit, is one, their glory is equal, and their majesty is co-eternal.

28 The three persons are one in being
The persons of the Trinity are inseparable in what they are and in what they do, but within the single divine operation each has a proper emphasis: the Father in his generation of all things, the Son in his Incarnation and the Holy Spirit in his work of sanctification.

29 The Father
By calling God 'Father' we confess two main things: a) that God is the source of every-

thing and the authority over all and b) that he is at the same time good and loving to all his children.

30 The Almighty

God is almighty. Nothing is impossible with God. He can do whatever he wills. He is the Creator and Lord of the universe, the order of which he established and which remains wholly subject to him and at his disposal. He is master of history, governing hearts and events in keeping with his will. In Christ's Resurrection and exaltation the Father has shown the immeasurable greatness of his power.

31 How everything was created

Creation is the work of the Holy Trinity. God the Father made all things by his Word and by his Wisdom, that is by his Son and by the Holy Spirit who, so to speak, are 'his hands'.

32 Creation's journey

The universe was not created in a finished state but 'in a state of journeying' toward the perfection to which God has destined it. We call the way God guides his creation toward this perfection 'divine providence'.

33 God allows us to work with him

God allows our co-operation in carrying out his plan. We have the dignity of being intelligent and free agents in completing the work of creation. We can co-operate with God through our actions, prayers and sufferings.

34 God permits evil

As intelligent and free creatures, angels and human beings have free choice. Through their own choices moral evil entered the world. God is never, directly or indirectly, the cause of moral evil. He permits it, however, because he respects the freedom of his creatures and knows how to derive good from it.

35 The Creator and his creation

God created the universe, freely, directly and without any help. He alone has the ability to call something into existence 'out of nothing' and it is he who keeps it in existence. He created the world to reveal his glory and so that his creatures could enjoy his truth, goodness and beauty.

36 The Creator of heaven

Angels, in nature, are spirits with intelligence and will. They are personal, immortal and more glorious than all visible creatures. With their whole beings the angels are servants of God. The word 'angel' means messenger.

37 The angels and us

Here on earth we share by faith in the blessed company of angels. We are surrounded by the watchful care and intercession of our guardian angels and in the liturgy we join with the angels to adore the thrice-holy God.

38 The Creator of earth

God made all things good. They reflect his wisdom in their internal stability and order. God's creatures were made interdependent, not self-sufficient. They live in the service of each other. Therefore we must respect all creation and not make wrong use of anything.

39 Man was made in the image of God

Of all visible creatures only man is made in the image and likeness of God and is able to know and love his Creator. He alone is called to share, by knowledge and love, in God's own life. It was for this end that man was created, and this is the basis of every individual's personal dignity.

40 With both body and soul
Man has a single nature made up of body and soul. Man's soul, the spiritual principle in him, is created immortal by God himself, not 'produced' by the parents. Man's body is the material world at its most perfect because in such a body the creature can freely praise the Creator. For this reason we may not despise our bodily life, rather we are to hold it in honour.

41 Man is both male and female
God created man, male and female, for each other. He created them distinct, equal, complementary and very good. Human harmony depends in part on the way men and women live out their complementarity. Therefore everyone should acknowledge and accept his or her sexual identity.

42 God is not in man's image
God is neither male nor female, but a pure

spirit. Yet the different 'perfections' of men and women, father and mother, reflect something of the infinite perfection of God.

43 Created in friendship with God

The first man was created in a state of friendship with his Creator and in harmony with himself and with the creation around him. He was not enslaved to any false desires.

44 The fall of the angels

Made by God, Satan, that is the devil, was at first a good angel, but he and other angels became evil by their own free choice to radically and irreversibly reject God and his reign.

45 The devil's power is limited

As a pure spirit, Satan is powerful. He can cause serious spiritual or physical injuries to human beings and to society. Still, he is only a creature and his power is limited. He cannot prevent the building up of God's kingdom.

46 The fall of man: disobedience

When the devil tempted man, saying he

could be like God, man abused his freedom and disobeyed God. In that sin – preferring himself to God and by that very act scorning him – man chose against his true nature as a creature and therefore against his own good.

47 The consequences of the fall

The first sin had tragic consequences:

- Adam and Eve became afraid of God and conceived a distorted image of him.
- Man's harmony with creation was broken.
- The union of man and woman became subject to tension, lust and domination.
- The control of the soul's spiritual faculties over the body was shattered.

48 Original sin

By his sin Adam lost the original holiness he had received from God, not only for himself but for all human beings. Adam and Eve transmitted to their descendants a weakened human nature that is inclined to sin, and subject to ignorance, suffering and death. This deprivation is called 'original sin'. Even so, our human nature is not totally corrupted but retains a measure of freedom and goodness.

49 God promises help

After the fall, man was not abandoned by God. On the contrary, God immediately announces the coming victory over evil. There is to be a 'New Adam' who, because of his obedience unto death, even death on a cross, will make amends for the disobedience of Adam and break the power of the evil one.

I believe in Jesus Christ, the only Son of God

50 His name: Jesus

We believe in Jesus, whose name in Hebrew means: 'God saves'. The name expresses both his identity and his mission. Since God alone can forgive sins, it is God, in Jesus his eternal Son made man, who 'will save his people from their sins'.

51 His name: Christ, the Messiah

The word 'Christ' is the Greek translation of the Hebrew 'Messiah', which means 'anointed'. It became the name proper to Jesus because he accomplished perfectly the divine mission of the Messiah, the hope of Israel, the one anointed to be priest, prophet and king.

52 His name: the Son of God

At his baptism and transfiguration Jesus is called the 'Beloved Son' by the Father. Jesus also calls himself the 'only Son of God', and by this title affirms that he has always existed. After his Resurrection, Jesus' divine sonship becomes manifest in the power of his glorified humanity.

53 His name: the Lord

By ascribing to Jesus the divine title 'Lord', we affirm that the power, honour and glory due to God the Father are due also to Jesus. We acclaim Christ as Lord over the world and over history, and recognize that we should submit to him as our master.

He was conceived by the Holy Spirit and born of the Virgin Mary

54 The Incarnation

The mystery of the Incarnation consists in the fact that the Son of God, the second person of the Trinity, assumed a human nature as Jesus of Nazareth – born to a daughter of Israel at Bethlehem in the time of King Herod the Great and the Emperor

Caesar Augustus – in order to accomplish our salvation.

55 Why the Word became flesh
The Word became flesh for us:
- to be our model of holiness as the way, and the truth, and the life,
- to heal our nature, and to make us 'partakers of the divine nature',
- to reconcile us with God so we can know his love,
- so that we would not perish but have eternal life.

56 True God
Jesus Christ is not part God and part man.* He became truly and fully human while remaining truly and fully God. Jesus Christ is true God and true man, two natures in one person, without confusion, change, division or separation.

---

* We confess that one and the same Christ, Lord, and only-begotten Son, is to be acknowledged in two natures without confusion, change, division or separation. The distinction between the natures was never abolished by their union, but rather the character proper to each of the two natures was preserved as they came together in one person (*prosopon*) and one hypostasis (*existence*).

57 How is the Son of God, man?

The second person of the Trinity, the Son, assumed our human nature, with a fully human soul, with all its operations of thought, emotion and will, and a fully human body. He is like us in all things except for sin.

58 Conceived by the Holy Spirit

The Holy Spirit, 'the Lord, the giver of Life', was sent to sanctify the womb of the Virgin Mary and cause her to conceive the eternal Son of the Father in a humanity drawn from her own.

59 Mary's virginity

Mary's virginity was real and perpetual* even in the act of giving birth to the Son of God made man. In fact, Christ's birth did not diminish his mother's virginal integrity but sanctified it. So the liturgy of the Church celebrates Mary as the 'Ever-virgin'.

---

*The 'brothers and sisters' to Jesus mentioned in the Bible have always been understood by the Church as not referring to other children of the Virgin Mary. James and Joseph, 'brothers of Jesus', are the sons of a woman whom St Matthew calls 'the other Mary'. They are close relations of Jesus, according to an Old Testament expression.

60 The Mother of God

Because the One conceived as the son of Mary is also the second person of the Holy Trinity, thus one person with two inseparable natures, all that happens to the man Jesus happens to the Son of God. Therefore the Church rightly calls Mary the 'Mother of God' (Theotokos).

61 The Immaculate Conception

For Mary to be able to give free assent to her vocation, it was necessary that she be 'full of grace' from God. From the first moment of her conception, by a singular grace and privilege of almighty God and by virtue of the merits of Jesus Christ, Saviour of the human race, she was preserved immune from all stain of original sin.

62 Christ's life is our model

Christ's whole earthly life – his words and deeds, his silences and sufferings, indeed his manner of being and speaking – is presented to us as our model. He is 'the perfect man', who invites us to become his disciples and follow him, to live in him so he can live in us.

63 Advent

Each Advent we celebrate the coming of Christ. His first historical coming, his Second Coming in glory and his personal coming to us individually.

64 Christmas

Jesus was born in a humble stable, into a poor family. Simple shepherds were the first witnesses to this event. In this poverty heaven's glory became visible. The Church never tires of singing the glory of this night, when we were made sharers in the divinity of Christ who humbled himself to share our humanity.

65 Epiphany

Epiphany celebrates the manifestation of Jesus as the Son of God and Saviour to the world. The three signal events recounted as epiphanies are the adoration of the magi, Jesus' baptism in the Jordan and the wedding feast at Cana.

66 The obedient 'New Adam'

By overcoming all temptation Jesus shows himself to be the devil's conqueror and the New Adam who remained faithful even unto death, whereas the first Adam did not. Because he is the New Adam, he makes a new human nature available to us from 'his fullness'.

67 Who put Jesus to death?

We should not blame the Jews in Jerusalem at the time for Jesus' death, much less other Jews of different times and places. All who have sinned, ourselves included, are guilty of causing Jesus' death. The guilt of Judas, the Sanhedrin, Pilate, and others is known to God alone.

68 In accordance with the Scriptures

The Scriptures foretold this divine plan of salvation that was to be accomplished through the putting to death of 'the righteous one' as a ransom to free us from the slavery of sin.

69 His death was a sacrifice

Christ's death is the true paschal sacrifice that accomplishes our definitive redemption. He is the Lamb of God, who takes away the sin of the world. His is the true blood of the covenant poured out for the forgiveness of sins. His offering is perfect.

70 He substitutes for us

Jesus, the Suffering Servant foretold by Isaiah, bore our sins and their punishment for our sake. Only Jesus, as a perfect human being, could atone for our faults and make satisfaction for our sins to the Father in substitution for us.

71 He died and was buried

Jesus, in his body, experienced the state of death, the separation of the soul from the body, between the time he died on the cross and the time he was raised from the dead, although his body saw no corruption due to its continued union with the divine Son.

He descended into hell and on the third day he rose again

72 His descent into hell*

Jesus descended into hell as the Saviour, proclaiming the Good News to the souls imprisoned there. Jesus did not deliver the damned, or destroy the hell of damnation, but freed the just who had gone before him.

73 The Resurrection on the third day

The crowning truth of our faith is the Resurrection of Jesus on the third day. Our faith is based on the eyewitness account of real people: Mary Magdalene and the holy women, Simon Peter, the Twelve, James and more than five hundred other persons. The Resurrection is a real event historically verified.

74 His resurrected body

Jesus' resurrected body is the same body that had been tortured and crucified. It bears the traces of his passion, yet it also possesses the new properties of a glorious body not limited by space and time.

*Hell is the translation of Sheol, the place where the dead wait, not Gehenna, the lake of fire.

75 Resurrection: the work of the Trinity

Christ's Resurrection is the work of the three divine persons acting together as one. The Father raised Christ from the dead, the Spirit gave life to Jesus' dead humanity and the Son, who laid down his life, took it up again.

76 The significance of the Resurrection

The Resurrection is the confirmation of all Christ's works and teachings. It was what he promised as the definitive proof of his divine authority. It is the basis of our justification. It reinstates us in God's favour as sons and daughters. It liberates us from sin and death and gives us a new and eternal life.

He ascended into heaven and is seated at the right hand of the Father

77 He ascended into heaven

Christ's Ascension marks the definitive entrance of Jesus' humanity into God's heavenly domain, where he intercedes for those who draw near to God through him. There he is hidden from our eyes until he comes in glory.

78 Seated at the right hand of the Father

The glory, honour and dominion of God is now given to the man Jesus Christ, who is seated at the right hand of the Father in his glorified flesh.

From thence he will come again to judge the living and the dead

79 He will come again in glory

At the end of the world, Christ will come in glory with the angels to achieve the final triumph of good over evil. Since the Ascension, Christ's coming in glory has been imminent. Only the Father knows the day and the hour; only he determines the moment of its coming.

80 In the meantime ...

Before Christ's second coming the Church must pass through a final trial and persecution that will shake the faith of many believers. The Antichrist will offer an apparent solution to all our problems, but at the price of rejecting the truth.

81 To judge the living and the dead

When he comes at the end of time to judge the living and the dead, Christ will reveal the secret disposition of our hearts and will give each of us what we deserve according to our works and according to our acceptance or refusal of grace.

I believe in the Holy Spirit

82 Belief in the Holy Spirit

To believe in the Holy Spirit is to profess that the Holy Spirit is one of the persons of the Holy Trinity, one in being with the Father and the Son. With the Father and the Son he is worshipped and glorified. The Holy Spirit proceeds from the Father as the source of all things, but also from the communion of the Father and the Son.

83 Encountering the Holy Spirit

The Holy Spirit manifests himself to us

- in Scripture, in Tradition and in the Magisterium,
- in the sacraments and in prayer,
- in the charisms and ministries of the Church,

- and in the saints.

84 The Holy Spirit is our helper
Jesus calls the Holy Spirit 'the Paraclete', which means 'he who is called to our side'. He is our advocate, helper, teacher, comforter, and counsellor.

85 Water is a symbol of the Spirit
Water signifies the Holy Spirit's action.
- In baptism it is a sign of new birth.
- Also, just as we must drink water to live, so we must drink of the one Spirit, the living water welling up in us, to have eternal life.

86 Anointing is a symbol of the Spirit
Anointing means to consecrate someone to fulfil an office. The Holy Spirit anointed Jesus in conception and baptism to be the Anointed One, the Messiah, and we are anointed to be like Jesus.

87 Other symbols of the Spirit
Other symbols of the Holy Spirit are fire, cloud, light, the seal, the hand or finger of God and the dove.

88 The Spirit prepares the way of the Lord

The Holy Spirit was preparing the way for the coming of the Lord through the law and the prophets, of whom John the Baptist is the last and greatest, because through John, the Spirit definitively identifies the Messiah, the one for whom all the prophets were searching.

89 The Spirit prepared Mary

For the first time in salvation history and because his Spirit had prepared her, the Father found a place where his Son and his Spirit could dwell with humanity. Through Mary, the Holy Spirit begins to bring human beings, the objects of God's merciful love, into communion with Christ.

90 Jesus pours out the Spirit

At the time of Pentecost, Christ's Passover is fulfilled in the outpouring of the Holy Spirit: manifested, given, and communicated as a divine person. On that day, the Holy Trinity is fully revealed.

91 The Spirit is a gift

God's gift of the Holy Spirit means his love is poured into our hearts. The first effects of this love are the forgiveness of sins and the restoration of the divine likeness. The Holy Spirit also gives us the first fruits of our inheritance: the very life of the Holy Trinity which gives us the ability to love others in God's own love.

I believe in the Holy Catholic Church

92 The meaning of 'Church'

The Church is the *ekklesia* (Greek) which means the assembly of people called apart for a religious purpose. In Christian usage the word 'church' designates the liturgical assembly, but also the local community and the whole universal community of believers. These three meanings are inseparable.

93 The Church was begun by Christ

The Church began when Jesus gathered his flock and taught them a new way of living and a prayer of their own. But it was at his death upon the cross that there came forth the 'wondrous sacrament of the whole Church' symbolized by the blood and water which flowed from the open side of the crucified Christ.

94 Christ structured the Church

The Lord gave the Church a structure that will remain until his Kingdom is fully achieved. He chose the Twelve with Peter as their head. Jesus entrusted a specific authority to Peter by giving him the keys of the kingdom of heaven. The 'power of the keys' designates authority to govern the house of God, which is the Church.

95 The Church is visible and invisible

Christ established and sustains his holy Church on earth as a *visible* organization through which he communicates truth and grace to all, but it is only 'with the eyes of faith' that one can see her *invisible* reality through which she is the bearer of divine life. The Church is essentially both human and divine, visible but endowed with invisible realities.

96 The mystery of the Church

The mystery of the Church is the mystery of Christ. God's plan was to unite all things to himself in Christ. Because the Church is the Bride of Christ, she is one with him and is thereby united with God. She responds in love to the gift of the Bridegroom who makes her holy.

97 The Church is a sacrament for all

The saving work of Christ is revealed and active in the Church's sacraments. They are the instruments by which the Holy Spirit distributes the grace of Christ to all. It is in this sense that the Church is called the universal sacrament of salvation.

98 The Church: the People of God

The Church is made up of a people: chosen by God, born anew by faith in Christ and baptism, in whom the Holy Spirit dwells, whose law is the new commandment to love as Christ loved us, whose mission is to be a light to the world and whose destiny is the Kingdom of God.

99 The Church: the Body of Christ

The Church is the Mystical Body of which Christ is the head: she lives from him, in him, and for him; he lives with her and in her. All her members are united with each other as a result of their union with Christ. Yet there is a diversity of members and functions.

100 The Church: a temple of the Holy Spirit

What the soul is to the human body, the

Holy Spirit is to the Body of Christ, the Church. Through the Spirit all the parts of the body are joined to each other and to their exalted head, for the whole Spirit of Christ is in the head, the whole Spirit is in the body, and the whole Spirit is in each of the members.

101 One, holy, catholic, apostolic

It is Christ who, through the Holy Spirit, makes his Church one, holy, catholic, and apostolic, and it is he who calls her to realize each of these qualities which she does not possess of herself.

102 The Church is one

The Church is one 1) because there is one Lord, one faith, one baptism, 2) because of her common celebration of divine worship, and 3) because of apostolic succession through the sacrament of Holy Orders which maintains unity in God's family.

103 The one and only Church of Christ

The one and only Church of Christ is that which our Saviour entrusted to Peter's pastoral care. This Church subsists in the

Catholic Church, which is governed by the successor of Peter and by the bishops in communion with him.

104 The one Church is divided

The Church experienced divisions from its very beginnings. One cannot charge those born into other Christian communities with the sin of the separation. Moreover, if they have been incorporated into Christ by faith and Baptism, they have a right to be called Christians, and to be accepted as brothers and sisters in the Lord.

105 God's grace outside the Church

Many elements of sanctification and of truth are found outside the visible confines of the Catholic Church: the written Word of God; the life of grace; faith, hope, and love, with the other interior gifts of the Holy Spirit, as well as other elements.

106 Working for Christian unity

Concern for achieving unity must involve the whole Church, the laity and clergy alike. Yet, this holy objective – the reconciliation of all Christians in the unity of the one and only Church of Christ – is beyond human power and ability. It is possible only in the power of the Holy Spirit.

107 The Church is holy

The Church is unfailingly holy because Christ gave himself up for her to make her holy and has endowed her with the gift of the Holy Spirit. Her holiness is real but imperfect. Perfect holiness is something yet to be acquired in her members; even so, through Christ the Church itself becomes sanctifying.

108 The saints

By canonizing some of the faithful as saints, i.e., by solemnly proclaiming that they practised heroic virtue and lived holy lives by God's grace, the Church gives her members models and intercessors. The saints have always been a source of renewal in the most difficult moments in the Church's history.

109 The Church is catholic

The Church is catholic – that is, universal – because she has received the fullness of the means of salvation: correct and complete confession of faith, full sacramental life, and apostolic succession. The Church is also universal because she has been sent out by

Christ on a mission to the whole of the human race.

110 Who belongs to the Church?

Those who accept all the means of salvation in, and the entire organization of, the Catholic Church are fully incorporated into it. The baptized who do not profess the entire Catholic faith are in a certain, but imperfect, communion with the Catholic Church. With the Orthodox Churches this communion is almost full.

111 The Church and the Jews

Unlike other non-Christian religions, Judaism is already a response to God's revelation in the Old Covenant. The Jewish people were the first to hear the Word of God and, according to the flesh, Christ was born of their race. God's call to them is irrevocable.

112 The Church and Muslims

God's plan of salvation also includes those who acknowledge the Creator, in the first place amongst whom are the Muslims; these profess to hold the faith of Abraham, and together with us they adore the one, merciful God, our judge on the last day.

113 The Church and non-Christians

The Catholic Church recognizes, in other religions, the search for the God who gives life, breath and all good things. The Church considers all goodness and truth found in these religions as a preparation for the Gospel given by him who enlightens all people that they might be saved.

114 Salvation outside the Church

Salvation only comes from Christ the Head and through his Body, the Church. Those who through no fault of their own do not know the Gospel of Christ, but who seek God with a sincere heart, and, moved by grace, try to do his will by following their conscience, may achieve eternal salvation.

115 The Church is missionary

Although God can bring those who are ignorant of the Gospel through no fault of their own to salvation, the Church still has the obligation and also the sacred right to preach the Gospel to every human being, having been sent by God to all the nations as the universal sacrament of salvation.

116 The Church is apostolic

The Church is apostolic because 1) she is built on the foundation of the apostles; 2) with the help of the Spirit she hands on the teaching she has heard from the apostles; and 3) she continues to be taught, sanctified, and guided by the apostles through their successors until Christ's return.

117 The Pope

The Pope is the perpetual and visible source of the unity of the bishops and of the whole company of the faithful. By reason of his office as Vicar of Christ, and as pastor of the entire Church, he has supreme and universal power over the Church, a power which he can always exercise unhindered.

118 The bishops together

The college of bishops exercises its power over the whole Church in an ecumenical council with the Roman Pontiff at its head. This college expresses the variety, the universality and the unity of the flock of Christ. Bishops may also meet with their neighbouring bishops in council.

119 Infallibility

To preserve the Church in the purity of the faith, Christ conferred on her a share in his own infallibility. The Roman Pontiff is infallible when he proclaims, by a definitive act, a doctrine pertaining to faith or morals. The infallibility given to the Church is also present in the body of bishops when, together with Peter's successor, they exercise the supreme Magisterium.

120 The bishop

The bishop is the visible foundation of unity in his own diocese. He exercises a pastoral, governing and teaching office over the People of God assigned to him. The faithful should respond with religious assent when he teaches in communion with the Pope on matters of faith and morals.

121 The bishop and his priests

By the sacred authority entrusted to them the bishop and his priests have the duty of authentically teaching the faith, celebrating divine worship, and guiding the Church as true pastors. They sanctify the Church by their prayer and work, by their ministry of the word and the sacraments, and by their example.

122 Lay people and the kingdom

The laity help establish the Kingdom of God by engaging in temporal affairs and directing them according to God's will. Their initiative is necessary especially for influencing social, political, and economic realities with Christian doctrine and life.

123 Lay people spread the faith

Lay Christians are entrusted by God with the call to spread the Kingdom of God. Through Baptism and Confirmation they have the ministry of priests, prophets and kings. They have the right and duty, individually or grouped in associations, to work so the message of salvation may be known and accepted by everyone on earth.

124 The laity are priests

The laity are priests in that they consecrate the world to God, offering worship by the holiness of their lives. Parents especially share in the office of sanctifying by leading a holy sexual life and by seeing to the Christian education of their children. Some lay people also assist in other 'priestly' ministries.

125 The laity are prophets

Lay people fulfil their prophetic mission by witnessing to their faith, in evangelization, in giving catechetical formation, in teaching the sacred sciences, and in use of the communications media. They have the right and at times a duty to manifest to the sacred pastors their opinion on matters which pertain to the good of the Church.

126 The laity are kings

The laity fulfil their kingly role by making their own body an obedient subject, by working to remedy the conditions of the world that lead people to sin and by functioning in positions of government in the world and the Church, e.g., in diocesan synods, pastoral councils, finance committees, ecclesiastical tribunals, etc.

127 Those in religious life

The 'religious life' is characterized by the public profession of the evangelical counsels of poverty, chastity, and obedience, in a stable state of life recognized by the Church. It is a special call to follow and imitate Christ more nearly. Those who are on this narrower path encourage the faithful by their example.

128 A communion of holy things

The communion of saints (*sancti*) refers first to the 'holy things' (*sancta*) held in common by the members of the Church, especially the sacraments and the charisms, but also their goods and their love. Everything held by the true Christian is to be regarded as a possession held in common with every other Christian.

129 A communion of holy people

The communion of saints refers also to the communion of 'holy persons' – all the faithful of Christ – those who are pilgrims on earth, the dead who are being purified, and the blessed in heaven. Together we form one Church. We share the same love of God and neighbour, and sing one hymn of glory to our God.

130 A communion of the living and dead

The saints who already dwell in heaven help establish the whole Church more firmly in holiness by their intercession for us. We on earth honour the dead by praying for them that they may be freed from their sins. Our prayer for them not only helps them, but also makes their intercession for us effective.

131 Mary, Mother of the Church

By her complete obedience to the Father's will, to the Son's redemptive work, and to every prompting of the Holy Spirit; by her obedience, faith, hope, and love; Mary is the Church's model and a mother to us in the order of grace. Her role does not obscure or diminish the unique mediation of Christ, but rather shows its power.

132 Devotion to Mary

Devotion to the Blessed Virgin is proper to Christian worship. The Church rightly honours the Blessed Virgin with special devotion that differs from the adoration which is given to God alone. The liturgical feasts dedicated to her and Marian prayers express this devotion to the Virgin Mary.

133 The Assumption of Mary

Because she was preserved free from original sin, the Virgin Mary, at the end of her earthly life, was taken up body and soul into heaven. The Assumption of the Blessed Virgin is a singular participation in her Son's Resurrection and an anticipation of the resurrection of all other Christians.

134 The forgiveness of sins in Baptism

Baptism is the first and chief sacrament of forgiveness of sins because it unites us with Christ, who died for our sins and rose for our justification. Baptism removes the stain of original sin and all other sins, but it does not deliver us from all the weaknesses of our human nature.

135 The forgiveness of sins in Confession

By Christ's will, the Church possesses the power to forgive the sins of the baptized and exercises this power through bishops and priests, normally in the sacrament of Penance. There is no offence, however serious, that the Church cannot forgive.

I believe in the resurrection of the body

136 What is death?

Death is the consequence of sin and the end of earthly life. It is the end of the time of grace and mercy which God offers us to work out our salvation and determine our own ultimate destiny. When our earthly life is completed, we shall not return to other earthly lives. There is no 'reincarnation' after death.

137 The resurrection of the body

By death the soul is separated from the body. But God, the Creator and the Redeemer of our flesh, will fulfil both the creation and the redemption of the flesh in the resurrection of the flesh. Just as Christ is risen and lives for ever, so all of us will rise at the last day and receive incorruptible life in our body, transformed by its reunion with our soul.

138 The meaning of Christian death

Because of Christ, Christian death has a positive meaning. Through baptism, the Christian has already 'died with Christ' sacramentally. If we physically die in Christ's grace, death completes this 'dying with Christ' and fully incorporates us into him.

139 Preparing for death

The Church encourages us to prepare ourselves for our own death. In the litany of the saints she has us pray: 'From a sudden and unforeseen death, deliver us, O Lord.' We also ask the Mother of God to intercede for us 'at the hour of our death'. Our every action and thought should be those of one who expects to die before the day is out.

I believe in life everlasting

140 Every person will be judged

Each of us will receive our eternal reward in our immortal soul at the very moment of our death in *the particular judgement* that relates to our life in Christ. The result is either entrance into the blessedness of heaven (immediately or through a purification) or immediate and everlasting damnation.

141 Life everlasting in heaven

If we die in God's grace, we will live for ever with Christ in heaven, which is the fulfilment of our deepest longings and a state of supreme, definitive happiness. We will become like God, for we will see him as he is, face to face. This is known as the beatific vision.

142 Purgatory

All who die in God's grace, but are still imperfectly purified, undergo purification, so as to achieve the holiness necessary to enter the joy of heaven. The Church calls the purification and the pardon in the age to come, as spoken of in Scripture, as 'purgatory'.

143 Hell

We cannot be united with God unless we freely choose to love him. We cannot love God if we sin seriously. Dying in mortal sin without repenting means remaining separated from God and happiness, for ever. This state of definitive self-separation from God is called 'hell'. God predestines no one to suffer the punishments of hell.

144 The last judgement

When Christ returns in glory the dead shall be raised and the Last (or general) Judgement will come. Christ will pronounce the final word on all history, making known the ultimate meaning of the whole work of creation, of the entire economy of salvation and the marvellous ways by which his Providence led everything towards its final end.

145 A new heaven and a new earth

At the end of time the Kingdom of God will come in its fullness. The universe itself, which attains its destiny through man, will be renewed. God's plan is to bring all things under the headship of Christ. There will be a new heaven and a new earth and God will have his dwelling among men.

146 The Amen

The Creed, like the last book of the Bible, ends with the Hebrew word *amen*. In Hebrew, 'amen' comes from the same root as the word 'believe'. Thus the Creed's final amen repeats and confirms its first words: 'I believe'. I believe, therefore I trust that God and his truth are completely reliable. Amen!

Part Two

The Sacraments

The Liturgy

147 What is liturgy?

In the liturgy Jesus Christ exercises his priestly office of offering public worship to God as the head of his Mystical Body. We participate both by joining in that offering and benefiting from it, as Christ continues the work of redemption in, with, and through his Church.

148 The liturgy and the Holy Trinity

In the liturgy the Father is acknowledged and adored as the source and the end of every blessing, and the Son fills us with the blessings of the Father and pours into our hearts the Gift that contains all gifts, the Holy Spirit.

149 The Father and the liturgy

The Father is the source and goal of the liturgy. The whole of God's work is a *blessing*: creation, the Passover, the Exodus, the giving of the law. In the liturgy we recall the Father's blessings and at the same time respond to them with blessings of praise and thanksgiving.

150 Christ and the liturgy

In the liturgy of the Church, Christ makes present his own paschal mystery. His paschal mystery is a real event that occurred in our history, but it cannot remain only in the past, since all that Christ is, participates in eternity, and so transcends time while being made present to all times.

151 How Christ is with us in the liturgy

Christ is always present in his Church's liturgical celebrations. He is present in the Mass especially in the Eucharistic species. He is present in the sacraments in the person of his minister. He is present in the reading of the Scriptures because he is the Word, and he is present whenever the Church prays.

152 The Holy Spirit and the liturgy

The mission of the Holy Spirit in the liturgy of the Church is to prepare the assembly to encounter Christ. The Holy Spirit also makes Christ and his saving work present to us. Through the work of the Spirit we are transformed and brought into communion with the Trinity and one another.

153 The purposes of the sacraments

The sacraments are signs (words and actions we can see and hear) instituted by Christ and entrusted to the Church, which actually present the grace that they signify, sanctifying those who receive them. They build up the Body of Christ and give worship to God. They not only presuppose faith, but also strengthen and express it.

154 Faith and the sacraments

In the liturgy the Holy Spirit bestows faith on the People of God. When the Spirit encounters in us the right response of faith, he brings about genuine co-operation: the liturgy becomes the common work of the Holy Spirit and the Church.

155 Christ gave us seven sacraments

The seven sacraments instituted by the Lord are: Baptism, Confirmation or Chrismation, Eucharist, Penance, Anointing of the Sick, Holy Orders, and Matrimony.

156 We celebrate the sacraments together

Christ empowered the apostles and their successors to act in his name and in his person. The ordained minister ties our liturgical actions to the apostles and, through them, to Christ. Yet it is the whole community, the Body of Christ united with its Head, that celebrates the sacraments.

157 Sacrament and Tradition

When the Church celebrates the sacraments, she confesses the faith received from the apostles. Liturgy is an essential element of Tradition. Therefore no sacramental rite may be modified or manipulated at the will of the minister or the community. Even the supreme authority in the Church may not change the liturgy arbitrarily.

158 How the sacraments work

The sacraments are effective because in them Christ himself is at work. The sacraments impart grace *ex opere operato* (by the very fact of their being done). The effectiveness of the sacrament does not depend on the righteousness of the celebrant, although the fruits of the sacrament do depend on the disposition of the recipient.

159 The sacraments and salvation

The Church affirms that for believers the sacraments are necessary for salvation. Those who receive sacramental grace are transformed into sons and daughters of God by the Holy Spirit. They become partakers in the divine nature by their union with the Son of God.

160 Sacraments and the heavenly liturgy

Whenever we celebrate the mystery of salvation in the sacraments we join with the angels, the patriarchs, the apostles, the saints, the martyrs, and all creation in the service of the praise of God. We participate in the eternal liturgy of heaven.

161 Sign, symbol and sacrament

Human beings use signs and symbols, language, gestures, and actions to communicate with others. The same holds true for our relationship with God. We express and perceive spiritual realities through physical signs and symbols we use in the sacraments.

162 Sources of signs and symbols

A sacramental celebration uses signs and symbols from:

- creation: light and darkness, fire and water;
- the social life of man: washing, breaking bread and sharing the cup; and
- the Old Covenant: laying on of hands, sacrifices, and above all the Passover.

163 Words and actions in the sacraments

The Word of God is an essential part of sacramental celebrations. This is emphasized by the veneration of the book containing the Word, its audible and intelligible reading, the minister's homily which extends its proclamation, and the response of the assembly in acclamation and thanksgiving.

164 The purpose of singing and music

Song and music are an integral part of a solemn liturgy. They fulfil their purpose of glorifying God and sanctifying the faithful according to three principal criteria: their beauty, their suitability to the occasion and the unity of participation by the assembly.

165 Sacred images
Sacred images in our churches and homes are intended to awaken and nourish our faith in the mystery of Christ. In icons and statues of Christ, it is he whom we adore. Through sacred images of the holy Mother of God, the angels and saints, we venerate the persons represented.

166 Sacred time: the Lord's Day
The Church celebrates the Resurrection every Sunday, the Lord's Day. It is the memorial of the first day, the day of creation, and the eighth day, the day that knows no evening. It is the pre-eminent day of liturgical assembly, the day of the Christian family, and the day of joy and of rest from work.

167 The liturgical year
In the course of the year the Church unfolds the whole mystery of Christ from his Incarnation and Nativity through his Death, Resurrection and Ascension, to Pentecost and the expectation of the blessed hope of the coming of the Lord.

168 The cycle of feasts

Easter holds a pre-eminent place as the 'Feast of feasts,' because the Resurrection is the culmination of Christ's work on earth. The cycle of feasts surrounding the mystery of the Incarnation (Annunciation, Christmas, Epiphany) are also noteworthy because they commemorate the beginning of our salvation.

169 Saints' feast days

By keeping the memorials of the saints – first of all the holy Mother of God, then the apostles, the martyrs, and other saints – we give glory to Christ for having accomplished his salvation in his glorified members, and their example encourages us on our way to the Father.

170 The daily prayer of the Church

The Liturgy of the Hours (the Divine Office) is intended to be the prayer of the whole People of God. Through it the faithful are united to Christ by praying the psalms, the canticles and blessings and by meditation on the Word of God.

171 **Sacred space**
Although churches are sacred, worship is not tied exclusively to them. The whole earth is sacred. Whenever and wherever the faithful assemble in prayer, they are 'living stones' built into a 'spiritual house'.

172 **The church building**
A church ought to be a place worthy of sacred ceremony. In entering a church we cross a *threshold*, symbolizing our passing from the world into the house of God. The parts of a church include: 1) the altar, 2) the tabernacle, 3) the chair of the bishop (or priest), 4) the pulpit, 5) the baptistry, and 6) the confessional.

173 **Liturgical diversity**
The mystery celebrated in the liturgy is one, but the forms of its celebration vary. These forms have arisen because of the Church's mission to all people of all cultures. The catholicity of the Church is manifested in the liturgical rites presently in use: the Latin, Byzantine, Coptic, Syriac, Armenian, Maronite and Chaldean. All of these rites are of equal dignity.

The Sacraments of Christian Initiation

174 The Sacraments of Christian Initiation

The sacraments of Christian initiation – Baptism, Confirmation, and the Eucharist – lay the foundations of every Christian life. In a way similar to the origin, development, and nourishing of natural life, the faithful are born anew by Baptism, strengthened by the sacrament of Confirmation, and receive in the Eucharist the food of eternal life.

The Sacrament of Baptism

175 Baptism

Baptism is the gateway to life in the Spirit, and the door to the other sacraments. Through Baptism we are freed from sin and reborn as sons of God; we become members of Christ, are incorporated into the Church and are made sharers in her mission.

176 Why do we call it Baptism?

This sacrament is called *Baptism*, after the central rite by which it is carried out: to baptize. In Greek *baptizein* means to immerse in water. Our immersion symbolizes burial into Christ's death, from which we rise up with him in his Resurrection as a new creature.

177 Baptism in the Old Testament

Baptism is prefigured:

- by water as a source of life;
- by Noah's ark, for in it eight persons were saved through water;
- by the crossing of the Red Sea. Israel was liberated from slavery to Egypt and we are liberated from slavery to sin; and
- by the crossing of the Jordan into the promised land. So, too, we cross into eternal life.

178 Joining the Christian people

Becoming a Christian is accomplished by a process of initiation. Certain essential elements always have to be present: proclamation of the Word leading to conversion, the profession of faith, Baptism itself, the outpouring of the Holy Spirit, and admission to Eucharistic communion.

179 The baptismal rite begins

The baptismal rite begins with the sign of the cross, which marks us as belonging to Christ and signifies our redemption by his cross. The proclamation of the Word of God enlightens the assembly with the truth and elicits the response of faith. In the exorcisms,

Satan is renounced and then the faith of the Church is confessed.

180 How we baptize

Baptism proper is done by triple immersion in water or by pouring water three times over the candidate's head. In addition, the baptized is anointed with sacred chrism, signifying the gift of the Holy Spirit, dressed in a white garment symbolizing that he or she has 'put on' or risen with Christ, and given a candle to show the world the light of Christ.

181 Baptism of adults

Adult Baptism is common where the proclamation of the Gospel is still new. Preparation for Baptism should include initiation in the doctrine of the Church, an understanding of its liturgical life, and the practice of virtue.

182 Baptism of children

Infant Baptism probably began among the earliest Christians when whole households received Baptism. God's generous grace of salvation is particularly manifest in infant Baptism. Born with a fallen human nature and tainted by original sin, children receive eternal life in Baptism and are freed from the power of darkness, having done nothing to earn it.

183 Faith and Baptism

Baptism is *the* sacrament of faith. The faith required for Baptism is not a perfect and mature faith, but a beginning. All the baptized, children or adults, must grow in faith *after* Baptism. For this reason each year the Church celebrates the renewal of baptismal promises at the Easter Vigil.

184 The community of faith

It is only within the faith of the Church that the faithful can believe. For the grace of Baptism to unfold, the faith and help of the parents, the godfather and godmother (who must be firm believers), and the whole Church, is important.

185 Who can baptize?

The ordinary ministers of Baptism are the bishop and priest and, in the Latin Church, the deacon. In case of necessity, anyone, even a non-baptized person, with the required intention, can baptize, by using the Trinitarian baptismal formula. The required intention is to will to do what the Church does when she baptizes.

186 The necessity of Baptism

Baptism is necessary for salvation for those to whom the Gospel has been proclaimed and who have had the possibility of asking for this sacrament.* The Church does not know of any means other than Baptism that assures entry into heaven. God has bound salvation to the sacrament of Baptism, but he himself is not bound by his sacraments.[†]

187 Forgiveness: the grace of Baptism

Original sin, all personal sins, and all punishment for sin are forgiven by Baptism. In those reborn, nothing remains that would impede their entry into the Kingdom of God. Yet Baptism does not remove all suffering, illness, death, weaknesses of character or the inclination to sin.

*The desire for baptism brings about the fruits of baptism in those who have not yet received it. Likewise those who suffer death for the sake of the faith without having received baptism are baptized by their death for and with Christ. (CCC\S 1258–1260)

[†]Children who have died without baptism must be entrusted to the mercy of God with reasonable hope, because of God's desire that all men should be saved, and Jesus' tenderness toward children. (CCC\S 1261)

188 Baptism makes us a new creation

Baptism also makes us 'a new creature', a child of God, a partaker of the divine nature, and a temple of the Holy Spirit. Baptism confers the grace of justification; it enables faith, hope and love, and provides the power to live the Christian life.

189 Baptism joins us to Christ

Baptism makes us members of the Body of Christ, members one of another, and it incorporates us into the Church, where we are called to be subject to others, to serve, obey and submit to the Church's leaders, holding them in respect and affection.

The Sacrament of Confirmation

190 We join the Church fully

Confirmation is necessary for the completion of baptismal grace. This sacrament initiates the baptized fully into the Church and enriches them with a special strength of the Holy Spirit.

191 Christ gave us this sacrament

Christ fulfilled his promise to pour out the Holy Spirit, first on Easter Sunday and then more strikingly at Pentecost. Thereafter, the apostles imparted, by the laying on of hands, the gift of the Spirit that completes the grace of Baptism. This is the origin of the sacrament of Confirmation.

192 The seal of Confirmation

A seal is a symbol of a person and a sign of authority or ownership. In Confirmation we are anointed with chrism which is the seal of the Holy Spirit. This seal marks our total belonging to Christ, our enrolment in his service for ever. Like Baptism, Confirmation imprints a spiritual mark on the soul; for this reason one can receive these sacraments only once.

193 How we celebrate Confirmation

Confirmation follows the renewal of the baptismal promises by those to be confirmed. The bishop performs the essential rite of Confirmation, anointing the confirmands with chrism on the forehead and saying the words: Be sealed with the Gift of the Holy Spirit.

194 The grace of Confirmation

Confirmation brings an increase of baptismal grace by 1) rooting us more deeply in the divine Sonship; 2) uniting us more firmly to Christ; 3) increasing the gifts of the Holy Spirit in us; 4) perfecting our bond with the Church; and 5) giving us a new strength to spread and defend the faith.

195 Candidates for Confirmation

A candidate for Confirmation who has attained the age of reason must profess the faith, be in a state of grace, have the intention of receiving the sacrament, and be prepared to assume the role of disciple and witness to Christ, both within the Church and the world. Every baptized person not yet confirmed can and should receive the sacrament of Confirmation.

The Sacrament of the Eucharist

196 Christ gave us the Eucharist

At the Last Supper our Saviour instituted the Eucharist to extend the sacrifice of the cross until he comes again. He entrusted the Eucharist to the Church as a memorial of his death and resurrection, as a sacrament of love and unity, and as a foretaste of the eternal paschal banquet.

197 The importance of the Eucharist

The miracles of the multiplication of the loaves and the water turned into wine prefigured the superabundance of the Eucharist. The Eucharist is the source and summit of the Church's life. It contains the whole spiritual good of the Church, namely Christ himself.

198 Other names for the Eucharist

The richness of the Eucharist is expressed in the different names we give it: Holy Communion, the Lord's Supper, Holy Mass, the Holy Sacrifice, the Most Blessed Sacrament, the Holy and Divine Liturgy, the Breaking of Bread, the memorial of the Lord's Passion and Resurrection, the Bread of Angels, Bread from Heaven, Medicine of Immortality, and the Viaticum.

199 The signs of bread and wine

The signs of bread and wine signify the goodness of creation. The bread reminds us of the offering of Melchizedek, of the unleavened bread of the Passover, and of the manna in the desert. The wine signifies festive joy and reminds us of the cup of blessing at the Jewish Passover.

200 Parts of the Mass

The Mass's structure, preserved throughout the centuries, includes:

- the liturgy of the Word, with the readings, homily and intercessions;
- the liturgy of the Eucharist, with the offering of the bread and wine, the consecratory thanksgiving, and communion.

The liturgy of the Word and the liturgy of the Eucharist form one act of worship.

201 The Eucharist and thanksgiving

Eucharist means 'thanksgiving'. In the Eucharist the Church presents all creation to the Father through the death and the Resurrection of Christ in thanksgiving that God has made it all good, beautiful, and just. The Eucharist is also the sacrifice of praise which sings the glory of God in the name of all creation.

202 The Eucharist and remembering

The Eucharist is the sacrificial memorial of Christ's Passover. The liturgical celebration does not just recollect past events; the proclamation of the works of God makes these events present and real. Therefore the Eucharist is a sacrifice because it *re-presents* the sacrifice of the cross.

203 The Eucharist and sacrifice

The Eucharist is the sacrifice of the Church. As the Body of Christ she is offered with her Head in one single sacrifice. In the Eucharist the lives of the faithful, their praise, sufferings, prayer, and work, are united with those of Christ and with his total offering, and so acquire a new value.

204 Transubstantiation

Christ is present most especially in the Eucharistic species and in a unique way. From the moment of consecration the whole Christ is truly, really, and substantially present in each of the Eucharistic species and in each part, and remains present as long as the species subsist. This change is fittingly called 'transubstantiation'.

205 Adoration of the Eucharist

We express our faith in the real presence of Christ under the Eucharistic species by genuflecting or bowing deeply as a sign of adoration of the Lord, by reserving the consecrated hosts with the utmost care, by exposing them to the solemn veneration of the faithful, and by carrying them in procession.

206 Preparing for Mass

We prepare ourselves for so great and so holy a moment by observing the required fast, examining our conscience, acknowledging our unworthiness, and conveying the respect, solemnity, and joy of this moment by our gestures and the way we are dressed.

207 Who offers the sacrifice of the Mass?

In the Eucharist, Christ pours out the grace of salvation on his Church. It is Christ himself, the eternal high priest who, acting through the ministry of the priest, offers the Eucharistic sacrifice. Only validly ordained priests can preside at the Eucharist and consecrate the bread and the wine.

208 Our obligation

We are obliged to go to Mass on Sundays and Holy Days, and – prepared by the sacrament of Reconciliation – to receive the Eucharist at least once a year, if possible during the Easter season. The Church strongly encourages us to receive the Eucharist on Sundays, feast days, or even daily.

209 The fruit of the Mass: union

Holy Communion preserves, increases, and renews the life of grace received at Baptism. It unites us more intimately with Christ Jesus, cleanses us from past sins and helps preserve us from future sins.

210 The fruit of the Mass: unity

Those who receive the Eucharist are united more closely to Christ, and thereby united together into one body – the Church. Communion renews, strengthens, and deepens this incorporation into the Church.

211 Communion with Eastern Churches

Eastern Churches that are not in full communion with the Catholic Church possess true sacraments because of apostolic succession; therefore having communion together, given suitable circumstances and the approval of Church authority, is not merely possible but is encouraged.

212 Intercommunion with Protestants

Ecclesial communities derived from the Reformation and separated from the Catholic Church have not preserved the proper reality of the Eucharistic mystery in its fullness, especially because of the absence of the sacrament of Holy Orders. For this reason Eucharistic intercommunion with these communities is not possible.

The Sacraments of Healing

213 The sacraments of healing

The Lord Jesus Christ, physician of our souls and bodies, has willed that his Church continue his work of healing and salvation. This is the purpose of the two sacraments of healing: the sacrament of reconciliation and the sacrament of Anointing of the Sick.

The Sacrament of Reconciliation

214 This sacrament is also called …

The sacrament of Reconciliation is also called the sacrament of Conversion, the sacrament of Penance, the sacrament of Confession and the sacrament of Forgiveness.

215 Our ongoing conversion

The new life received in Christian initiation does not instantly perfect us in holiness. Our ongoing conversion is necessary. The Lord has given us the sacrament of Penance as a way for this to happen. In it the Holy Spirit convicts us of the horror of sin and makes our hearts return to the Lord and then gives us the strength to begin anew.

216 Christ gave us this sacrament

In giving Simon Peter the keys of the kingdom of heaven and the power to bind and loose, Christ gave the apostles and their successors the power to forgive sins and to reconcile sinners with God and the Church. Reconciliation with the Church is inseparable from reconciliation with God.

217 Confession and the law of the Church

Sacramental confession must be made to a priest and regular confession is strongly recommended by the Church. Anyone aware of having committed a mortal sin must not receive Holy Communion without first receiving sacramental absolution, unless there is a serious reason for an exception. Children must make their first confession before their first Holy Communion.

218 The two parts of this sacrament

The sacrament of Reconciliation has two equally essential parts:

- the acts of the penitent through the intervention of the Holy Spirit; namely, contrition, confession and satisfaction;
- God's action through the intervention of the Church to forgive sins in the name of Jesus Christ, to determine the penance, and to pray for the sinner.

219 How we go to Confession

The sacrament of Reconciliation ordinarily involves a greeting and blessing from the priest, a reading from the Word of God to illuminate the conscience, a call to repentance, confession, a penance, the priest's absolution, a prayer of thanksgiving and praise, and the dismissal with the blessing of the priest. In cases of grave necessity general confession and absolution are permitted.

220 Being sorry for our sins

Proper preparation for confession is made by an examination of conscience based on the Word of God. True repentance requires the sinner to be sorry for and to detest the sin committed, and to have the resolution not to sin again.

221 Confession

Confession of sins frees us from their power. Through confession we look squarely at the sins we are guilty of and take responsibility for them. We thereby open ourselves again to God and to reconciliation with others. Knowingly withholding some sins makes our confession invalid.

222 The confessional powers of priests

Priests, by virtue of the sacrament of Holy Orders, have the power to forgive all sins. The priest is not the master of God's forgiveness but its servant, and should unite himself to the intention and charity of Christ. He must pray and do penance for the penitent and is bound to keep absolute secrecy regarding sins confessed to him.

223 Making up for what we did wrong

Many sins wrong our neighbour. One must do what is possible to repair the harm. But sin also injures and weakens the sinner, and absolution does not remedy all the disorders sin has caused. The sinner must still recover full spiritual health by doing the penance imposed by the confessor.

224 Forms of penance

The three most important forms of penance – fasting, prayer, and almsgiving – express conversion in relation to oneself, to God, and to others. They are particularly appropriate for times like Lent, and every Friday. Also appropriate are various types of spiritual exercises, voluntary self-denial, and charitable works.

225 The fruit of this sacrament

Through this sacrament we are reconciled with God, ourselves, our brethren, the Church, and all creation. This reconciliation usually brings a sense of peace and spiritual consolation. It increases our strength for the spiritual battle. It restores our dignity and revitalizes the Church. It also acquits us of eternal punishment due to mortal sin and affords us the remission, at least in part, of temporal punishment.

226 Indulgences

An indulgence is a pardon of the temporal punishment due to us for sins the guilt of which has already been forgiven. Indulgences are gained for oneself or for those in purgatory through actions prescribed by the Church and can be either partial or full.

The Sacrament of the Anointing of the Sick

227 Christ gave us this sacrament

Jesus shared his ministry of healing with the twelve and gave them authority to heal disease and infirmity. The apostolic Church already had its own rite for the sick, attested to by St James.

228 How we anoint the sick

The Anointing of the Sick may be done for one sick person or a whole group in a home, hospital or church. It normally includes an act of repentance, a reading from Scripture, the laying on of hands in prayer, and anointing on the forehead and hands with oil blessed by the bishop.

229 Why we anoint the sick

The purpose of the sacrament of the Anointing of the Sick is to confer a special grace on us when we experience the difficulties inherent in serious illness or impending death. Each time we fall seriously ill, or when an illness worsens or we face death, we may receive the Anointing of the Sick.

230 Preparing for death

The Church offers the Eucharist as viaticum to those who are about to leave this life. It is the seed of eternal life and the power of resurrection. Thus Penance, the Anointing of the Sick and the Eucharist are the sacraments that help us to end our earthly life well.

231 The fruit of the Sacrament of the Sick

The Sacrament of the Anointing of the Sick has as its effects: 1) the uniting of the sick person to the Passion of Christ; 2) the imparting of strength, peace, and courage to endure the sufferings of illness or old age; 3) the forgiveness of sins; 4) the restoration of health; and 5) the preparation for passing over to eternal life.

The Sacraments at the Service of Communion and Mission

The Sacrament of Holy Orders

232 What do the words 'Holy Orders' mean?

Since ancient times the Church has had orders: bishops, priests, deacons, catechumens, virgins, spouses, widows. Today the words 'Holy Orders' and 'ordination' are reserved for the sacramental act which makes a man a bishop, priest, or deacon.

233 The one priesthood of Christ

Christ, *the* high priest, has made the Church a kingdom of priests. The faithful are consecrated to be a holy priesthood through the sacraments of Baptism and Confirmation. Together with the bishops and priests all the faithful participate in the one priesthood of Christ.

234 Christ gave us this sacrament

From the beginning of his ministry, the Lord Jesus instituted the Twelve as a sacred hierarchy to shepherd the People of God and to increase their number until the end of time. Those invested with this sacred power are dedicated to promoting the interests of their brethren, so that all who belong to the People of God may attain to salvation.

236 The priest represents Christ

By virtue of the sacrament of Holy Orders, the priest acts in the power and place of the person of Christ himself and makes the presence of Christ as Head of the Church visible. However, priests are not preserved from all human weaknesses or sin by this sacrament.

236 Bishops

A bishop receives the fullness of the sacrament of Holy Orders. He becomes a member of the college of bishops and the visible head of his diocese. In virtue of the unbroken apostolic succession, bishops are the transmitters of the faith, and they inherit the office of sanctifying, teaching and ruling.

237 Priests

Ministerial priesthood differs in essence from the common priesthood of the faithful. As the bishop's co-workers, priests bear responsibility with him for the diocese. They receive from the bishop the charge of a parish or a particular role in the diocese.

238 Deacons

Deacons are ordained to serve the Church as their bishop directs. Ordination confers on them limited but important functions in ministry: distributing Holy Communion, assisting at and blessing marriages, proclaiming the Gospel, preaching, presiding over funerals, providing pastoral governance, and carrying out charitable works.

239 Conferring the sacrament

This sacrament is conferred by a bishop laying on hands and saying a solemn prayer of consecration. It imprints an indelible character and confers, from Christ himself, a sacred power of service exercised in teaching, divine worship and pastoral governance.

240 Who can receive this sacrament?

No one has a *right* to receive Holy Orders. Only a baptized man can receive sacred ordination if authorized by the Church. The Lord Jesus chose men to form the college of the twelve apostles, and the Church recognizes herself to be bound, by the Lord's choice, not to ordain women.

241 Celibacy

The ordained ministers of the Latin Church, with the exception of permanent deacons, are normally chosen from among celibate men because they can give themselves entirely to God and to the people they serve. When accepted with a joyous heart, celibacy radiantly proclaims the Reign of God.

242 Not marrying for the sake of Christ

Christ himself has invited certain persons to follow him in his celibate way of life, of which he remains the model. Those who have renounced the great good of marriage to imitate Christ, to be intent on the things of the Lord, and to wait for him in prayer, show that love for Christ takes precedence over all other things.

The Sacrament of Matrimony

243 God created marriage

Marriage is not a purely human institution. The married state has been established by the Creator. It is an image of the absolute and unfailing love of God and is intended to be fruitful. Thus unity, indissolubility, and openness to fertility are essential to marriage.

244 Christ gave us this sacrament

Christ the Lord raised marriage between the baptized to the dignity of a sacrament. Jesus performed his first sign during a wedding feast. The Church attaches great importance to Jesus' presence at this wedding. She sees in it the confirmation of the goodness of marriage and Christ's presence in marriage.

245 Marriage and the Eucharist

Marriage between two Catholics normally takes place during Mass, the memorial of the New Covenant in which Christ united himself to the Church, his bride. By offering each other their lives in covenant during the Eucharist, the bride and groom become more perfectly one together and more perfectly one with Christ.

246 Conferring the sacrament

The spouses confer upon each other the sacrament of Matrimony. The partners formally give themselves to each other by expressing their consent before the Church. This is the indispensable element that makes the marriage. It must be an act of the will and free of external coercion.

247 Marriage and the law of the Church

The law of the Church regarding marriage says every marriage must be open to having children. It forbids polygamy, divorce, and remarriage during the lifetime of a lawful spouse. After an examination, the Church can declare the nullity of a marriage; i.e., that the marriage never existed.

248 Marrying a non-Catholic

A marriage between a Catholic and a baptized non-Catholic needs the express permission of the Church. Marriage to someone who is not baptized needs an express dispensation from the Church. To enter a mixed marriage, the Catholic party must make known and confirm the obligations of a) preserving his or her own faith and b) ensuring the Baptism and education of the children as Catholics.*

249 The grace of marriage

The sacrament of Matrimony bestows the grace for spouses to love each other with the love with which Christ has loved his Church. The sacrament thus perfects the human love of the spouses, strengthens their indissoluble unity, prepares them for welcoming and educating children and sanctifies them on the way to eternal life.

250 Expressing love as married people

Proper sexual love is not simply biological, but concerns the innermost being of the

---

*See your diocese's or country's common practice for mixed marriages and any decisions for a specific interpretation of what this means.

human person. It aims at a deeply personal unity of one flesh, one heart and soul. It is noble and honourable because it fosters self-giving, joy and gratitude.

251 Caring for the divorced

Divorced people who are remarried civilly, are in a situation that contravenes God's law. Consequently, they cannot receive Eucharistic communion, or exercise certain ecclesial responsibilities. Priests and the community must take concern for the divorced so that they do not become separated from the Church, in whose life they can and must participate.

252 The family is a little church

Believing families are centres of living, radiant faith: the domestic church. By their word and example parents are the first heralds of the faith to their children and should encourage their children in the calling in life which is proper to them, fostering with special care any religious vocation.

253 Single people

Single persons, because of the particular circumstances in which they live (often not of their choosing) are especially close to Jesus' heart. They deserve the special affection and active care of the Church. The doors of family homes must be open to all of them.

Other Liturgical Celebrations

254 Sacramentals

Sacramentals are sacred actions which prepare us to receive grace and dispose us to cooperate with it. Various occasions in life are rendered holy by them. Lay people may preside at many of them. Among sacramentals, blessings (of persons, meals, objects, and places) are of first importance.

255 Blessings

Blessings intended for persons include the blessing of an abbot or abbess, the consecration of virgins and widows, the rite of religious profession and the blessing of certain ministries of the Church (e.g., readers, altar servers, catechists). Blessings that concern objects include the dedication of a church or altar, the blessing of holy oils, vessels, vestments, bells, homes, etc.

256 Exorcism

Exorcism is the process of expelling demons from a person or an object. It includes prayers and rites to set them free and to protect them against the power of the Evil One through the spiritual authority Jesus entrusted to his Church. A solemn exorcism can be done only by a priest with the permission of his bishop.

257 Common forms of piety

Expressions of piety extend the liturgical life of the Church, but do not replace it. They must be supervised and kept free from error. Some common forms include retreats, pilgrimages to holy places, processions, the stations of the cross, religious dances, the rosary, wearing medals, the veneration of relics, etc.

258 Funerals

A funeral initiates the fulfilment of the sacramental life: the new birth to eternal life begun at Baptism, the conformity to Christ conferred by Confirmation, and the heavenly feast anticipated in the Eucharist.

259 The main parts of a funeral service

The four principal elements of a funeral are: a) a greeting of faith and comfort, b) the liturgy of the Word that illumines the mystery of Christian death, c) the Eucharist, expressing eternal communion with the departed, and d) a final commendation of the deceased to God by the Church.

Part Three

The Ten Commandments

Our Vocation

260 The Beatitudes

The Beatitudes express the actions and attitudes that should be characteristic of the Christian life and reveal our true vocation, the final end to which God calls us: the kingdom, the vision of God, participation in the divine nature, eternal life, restoration as sons and daughters of God, rest in God.

261 The dignity of the human person

Our dignity as human beings is rooted in being created in the image and likeness of God. God created us as rational beings, able to initiate and control our own actions. Because we have free will, we are moral beings. We are capable of directing ourselves toward what is true and good and thus increasing in perfection.

262 Our reason informs our will

By our reason, we are capable of understanding the order of things established by the Creator. By our reason, we recognize the voice of God which urges us to do what is good and avoid what is evil, but because of original sin, we are now inclined to evil and subject to error.

263 Freedom brings responsibility

Because we have free will, every act we directly will is the responsibility of the one who does it. Responsibility for an action and its effects can be diminished or even negated by ignorance, inattention, duress, fear, habit, excessive attachments, and other psychological or social factors.

264 The morality of human acts

Human acts can be good or evil (sinful) depending on the objective morality of the act, the intentions of the person acting, and the circumstances surrounding the action, including its after-effects.

265 Intentions and circumstances

Intentions and circumstances can increase or decrease the moral goodness or evil of human acts. However, neither a good intention nor a special circumstance can make an act that is objectively evil, good. (The end does not justify the means.) A bad intention does make a good act evil.

266 Passions and feelings

In themselves passions are neither good nor evil. They are morally good when they contribute to a good action, and evil when they contribute to an evil action. The passions are to be governed by reason and their proper use is part of moral perfection. They can be taken up into the virtues or perverted by the vices.

267 Conscience

Deep within us is a voice calling us to love good and to avoid evil. This is our conscience. It judges actions as good or evil. It recognizes the authority of truth and welcomes the commandments. We must actively listen to our conscience and faithfully do what we believe to be right.

268 Forming our conscience

The education of the conscience is a lifelong and indispensable task, but it guarantees freedom and peace of heart. In the formation of conscience we are helped by the Word of God, the gifts of the Holy Spirit, the advice of others, and the authoritative teaching of the Church.

269 Faulty judgements

Individuals may be responsible for the erroneous formation of their conscience if they have taken too little trouble to find out what is true and good or if they have rejected the Church's teaching.

270 The virtues forge our character

Human virtues are habits of thinking, feeling and acting that forge good character. They are gained through God's grace and human effort – by education, by deliberate acts and by perseverance.

271 Prudence

Prudence is the practical reasoning that helps us know our true good in every circumstance and the right means of achieving it. Prudence helps us judge true virtue from apparent virtue and helps us keep all the virtues in balance. One cannot be truly courageous, just or temperate without prudence.

272 Justice

Justice is the moral virtue of giving to God and neighbour their due. It disposes one to seek harmony in human relationships. It respects the rights of the individual while upholding the common good.

273 Fortitude

Fortitude gives us strength to resist temptation and to overcome obstacles in the moral life. It helps us to conquer fear, even fear of death, and to face trials and persecutions. It disposes us even to sacrifice our lives in defence of a just cause.

274 Temperance

Temperance is the moral virtue that helps us control the attraction of pleasures and gives us balance in the use of created goods. Through temperance we have mastery over our instincts and desires.

275 Faith

Faith is the first of the three theological virtues, that is, the virtues which have God for their origin, motive and object. Through the virtue of faith we believe in God and all that he has revealed to the Church. Faith deprived of hope and love does not fully unite the believer to Christ. Faith without works is dead.

276 Hope

Hope is the theological virtue which leads us to desire the eternal happiness of heaven. It also keeps us from discouragement, sustains us during times of abandonment, preserves us from selfishness, and helps us persevere in times of difficulty.

277 Love or charity

Charity is the theological virtue by which we love God above all things, and we love our neighbour as ourselves. Charity helps us obey all God's commandments and makes us able to love as Christ does, including even our enemies. Its fruits are joy and peace.

278 Love is the greatest of the virtues

Charity is kindness, benevolence, mercy, generosity, friendship and tolerance. It is the greatest of all the virtues because it inspires and enlivens all the others. The practice of charity produces Christian spiritual freedom.

279 The gifts of the Spirit

The gifts of the Holy Spirit are permanent dispositions which make us ready to follow the promptings of the Holy Spirit. The seven gifts of the Holy Spirit are wisdom, understanding, counsel, fortitude, knowledge, piety, and fear of the Lord.

280 The fruits of the Spirit

The fruits of the Spirit are the first fruits of eternal glory. The tradition of the Church lists twelve of them: charity, joy, peace, patience, kindness, goodness, generosity, gentleness, faithfulness, modesty, self-control, chastity.

281 Defining sin

Sin is an utterance, deed, or desire contrary to God's law. It is an offence against truth and a failure in love toward God and neighbour. Sin turns our hearts toward self-exaltation and wounds our nature.

282 The different kinds of sins

Sins are offences in thought, word, deed, or omission. They can be distinguished according to their motive and purpose, or the virtues they oppose, or the commandments they violate. They can also be classified according to whether they concern God, neighbour, or self.

283 The seven capital sins

All sins and vices can be classified under one or more of the seven capital or deadly sins. These seven sins are: pride, greed, envy, wrath, lust, gluttony, and sloth.

284 Sins differ in their seriousness

The gravity of sins varies. Mortal sin is a serious violation of God's law that destroys charity. For a sin to be mortal, three conditions must all be met: it must be seriously wrong, we must know it is seriously wrong and we must deliberately decide to do it.

285 Seriousness and fault

How serious a sin is depends on who is wronged: violence against parents is in itself more serious than violence against a stranger. Ignorance, passions, external pressures or pathological disorders can diminish or even remove responsibility for a serious offence.

286 Restoration from mortal sin

Without repentance and forgiveness, mortal

sin results in eternal death in hell. Such sins necessitate God taking a new initiative in his mercy to bring a conversion of heart that must be completed by going to confession.

287 Venial sin

One commits venial sin by disobeying the moral law in a less serious matter, or by disobeying the moral law in a serious matter but without full knowledge or without complete consent. Venial sin hinders the soul's progress, and deserves punishment.

288 Sin causes more sin

Sin tends to reproduce itself and reinforce itself. By repetition, sin becomes a vice; that is, a habit of committing a particular sin. Sin and vice confuse our conscience and damage our judgement.

289 Responsibility for others' sins

We bear responsibility for sins committed by others when we co-operate in them:

- by participating directly and voluntarily in them;
- by ordering, advising, praising, or approving them;

- by not disclosing or not hindering them when we should;
- by protecting evildoers.

290 Sinful structures
Sins give rise to social situations and institutions that are unjust. These 'sinful structures' are the expression and effect of personal sins. They lead their victims to do evil in their turn.

291 Communal responsibility
Our vocation is not just personal, but communal as well. Human nature requires us to live in society. Certain societies, such as the family and the state, correspond to our nature and are necessary for us. We owe loyalty to them, and should show them respect, with gratitude and goodwill.

292 Subsidiarity
A community of a higher order should not interfere in the internal life of a community of a lower order, but rather should support it in case of need and help to co-ordinate it with the rest of society. Excessive intervention by the state can threaten personal freedom and initiative.

293 The just hierarchy of values

Christians must work to support the just hierarchy of values in society, especially to see that they are respected in institutions and living conditions that are an inducement to sin. The just hierarchy of values places the physical and instinctual spheres below the interior and spiritual ones.

294 Authority is necessary

Every human community needs an authority to govern it to ensure the unity of the state and the common good of society. The choice of the form of government and the appointment of rulers belong to the citizens.

295 Just and unjust laws

Authority is exercised legitimately if it employs morally acceptable means. A human law is just in so far as it accords with right reason. In so far as it falls short of right reason it is said to be an unjust law and is not binding in conscience.

296 The common good

Those in government must keep three essential goods in mind:

- respect for human freedom and the indi-

vidual's basic human rights,
- the social well-being, the prosperity and the spiritual development of the group itself,
- peace, stability and security.

297 Human equality and differences

Because all human beings are created in the image of God and have a common nature with a rational soul, all of us are of equal dignity. All forms of social or cultural discrimination in basic personal rights on the grounds of sex, race, colour, social conditions, language, or religion are incompatible with God's design.

298 Human solidarity (harmony)

Solidarity is a very Christian virtue. It can be seen first in the distribution of goods and payment for work. It also presupposes the effort for a more just social order where tensions are reduced and conflicts settled by negotiation. It practises the sharing of spiritual goods even more than material ones.

299 The moral law

The moral law prescribes the rules of good

conduct that lead to happiness. It forbids the ways of evil, which turn us away from God and his love. The moral law finds its fullness and its unity in Christ, who is, in his person, the way of perfection.

300 Expressions of the moral law
The different expressions of the moral law are all interrelated: eternal law (the source of all law), natural law, revealed law (the Old and New Testaments), and finally, civil and church laws.

301 What is natural law?
Human beings have an inborn moral sense. We quickly recognize the same moral principles as true. These principles make up natural law. It defines good and evil, truth and falsehood, helping us know what we must and must not do.

302 Natural law is a basis for society
The natural law is universal, unchangeable and eternal. It states the first and essential precepts which govern the moral life and it provides a common moral foundation for every society's necessary civil laws.

303 Revealed law: the old law

The first stage of revealed law is summed up in the Ten Commandments which prohibit what is contrary to the love of God and neighbour and prescribe what is essential to it. The Old Law is holy, spiritual, and good, yet still imperfect. It shows what must be done, but does not give the strength to fulfil it.

304 The new law

The new revealed law is expressed in the Sermon on the Mount and in the moral teaching of the apostles. It is the work of the Holy Spirit who teaches us what must be done and gives us the grace through the sacraments to do it.

305 A law of love, grace and freedom

The Law of the Gospel is called:

- a law of love, since Jesus has showed us how to love and has enabled us to do it
- a law of grace, since it confers the grace we need to be able to act rightly
- a law of freedom, since it sets us free from the Old Testament rituals.

306 Grace

Grace is the free gift of God, by which he pours his own life into our soul through the Holy Spirit. By grace, through faith in Jesus Christ, and through baptism, we are justified: we are cleansed from our sins and given the righteousness of God. Individuals can reject the grace of God, but they cannot move toward justification without it.

307 Justification

Moved by grace, we can turn toward God and away from sin, accepting from on high the forgiveness and justification which heals, sanctifies and renews us. Through justification faith, hope, and charity are poured into our hearts and we become communicants in the divine nature and members of the Body of Christ.

308 Merit

Once justified we can merit for ourselves, and for others, the graces needed to grow in holiness, and for the attainment of eternal life. Even so, any merit we achieve is still due to God, for our good actions are done in Christ through the assistance given by the Holy Spirit.

309 Holiness

All Christians are called to perfection, to holiness, toward an ever more intimate union with Christ. This perfection increases through participation in the sacraments, but it also demands self-denial and a spiritual battle, as is clearly shown in the lives of so many saints.

310 The laws of the Church

The five precepts of the Church define what is necessary in prayer and moral effort for growth in holiness. The five precepts are:

- You shall attend Mass and rest from servile labour on Sundays and Holy Days of Obligation.
- You shall confess your sins at least once a year.
- You shall receive the Eucharist during the Easter season.
- You shall observe the established days of fasting and abstinence.
- You shall help to provide for the needs of the Church.

311 We are witnesses by our moral life

For the message of salvation to show the power of its truth, it must be demonstrated by Christians leading morally upright lives. Leading a moral life is also our response to the Lord. It is homage and thanksgiving given to God.

312 Special graces

Special graces, also called charisms or gifts, are given to us by God in service to the message of salvation and for the common good of the Church. These gifts differ according to the grace given to us and include: the gifts of miracles, tongues, prophecy, service, teaching, exhortation, liberality, etc.

The Ten Commandments

313 Our relationship with God

In establishing a covenant with us, God sets our relationship with him as the most important thing for us. By revealing the Ten Commandments in the context of establishing a covenant with us, God shows us that our moral behaviour is vital to that relationship. It is part of how we worship and honour God.

314 The law has not been abolished

By his life and by his preaching Jesus attested to the permanent validity of the Ten Commandments. In him, the law has not been abolished, rather it is perfectly fulfilled. Thus, Christians are still bound to keep the commandments, especially as interpreted in the light of the two-fold summary of Christ.

315 The nature of the Ten Commandments

The Ten Commandments reveal serious, permanent responsibilities that are binding on all people at all times. The commandments mutually condition one another. Thus, breaking one commandment is breaking the whole law.

The First Commandment

I am the LORD your God. You shall have no other gods before me. You shall not make for yourself a graven image; you shall not bow down to them or serve them. (Exodus 20: 2–5)

316 Worship is God's just demand

God's first call and just demand is that we accept him and worship him. When we say 'God' we confess a supreme being, unchanging, just, merciful, and good. It follows that we must accept his words, have complete faith in him, and acknowledge his authority.

317 Faith, hope and love

The first commandment is concerned with faith, hope, and love. It requires us to nourish and protect our faith, hope and love wisely and diligently, and to reject everything that is opposed to them.

318 Sins against faith in God

The obedience of faith is our first obligation. There are various ways of sinning against the obedience of faith, including refusing to believe what God has revealed, neglecting or rejecting one's faith, believing a false teaching, and participating in a schism in the Church.

319 Sins against hoping in God

Hope is the confident expectation of seeing God face to face. Sins against hope include despair and presumption. Despair is contrary to the goodness of God. Presumption mocks God's mercy.

320 Sins against the love of God

The first commandment enjoins us to love God above everything, and to love all creatures for him and because of him. One can sin against God's love through indifference, ingratitude, lukewarmness, laziness, and hatred of God.

321 Adoration of God

Adoration is God's due. To adore God is to acknowledge him as God: Creator, Saviour and Lord of everything that exists. We adore God by offering prayers of praise and thanksgiving, intercession and petition. We adore God simply because we would not exist but for him.

322 Promises and vows

Promises made in Baptism and Confirmation, Matrimony and Holy Orders, or made in personal devotion, should be faithfully kept. They are signs of our love and respect for a faithful God. Dedicating oneself to God with vows, especially of poverty, chastity and obedience, is also an act of worship.

323 We must not worship false gods

The first commandment condemns belief in

more than one God and all idolatry: the belief in or veneration of pagan gods. We also commit idolatry whenever we revere a created thing in place of God, whether this be gods or demons, power, pleasure, race, ancestors, the state, money, etc.

324 Veneration of images

The Christian veneration of images is not making images of false gods. The honour paid to sacred images is respectful veneration, not the adoration due to God alone. To venerate an image is to venerate the person portrayed in it.

325 We must not practise sorcery

All forms of divination are to be rejected: recourse to Satan or demons, mediums or psychics, conjuring up the dead, consulting horoscopes, astrology, palm reading, interpretation of omens and lots. Magic, sorcery or other attempts to tame occult powers are seriously wrong. Wearing charms is also reproachable.

326 We must not tempt God

The first commandment condemns tempting God, sacrilege, and simony.

- Tempting God in words or deeds wounds the respect and trust we owe him.
- Sacrilege is treating persons, actions, things, or places consecrated to God unworthily.
- Simony is buying or selling spiritual powers or privileges.

327 Atheism is wrong

Since it rejects or denies the existence of God, atheism is a sin against the first commandment. Practical materialism is atheism that restricts human needs to space and time or equates the liberation of man just with economic and social liberation. Atheistic humanism falsely considers man to be an end to himself.

328 Agnosticism is wrong

Agnosticism is the belief that the existence of God is impossible to prove or irrelevant. Agnosticism is often an expression of indifferentism and leads to a sluggish moral conscience.

The Second Commandment

You shall not take the name of the LORD your God in vain. (Exodus 20: 7)

329 Respect for what is holy

We must respect the Lord's name and use right speech in sacred matters. The abuse of the names of God, the Virgin Mary, the saints, Christ's Church, and all sacred things is blasphemy and is in itself a serious sin. We must not use words of hatred, reproach, or defiance against what is holy.

330 Oaths

To take an oath is to call God as witness that what one is saying is true and most reliable. Oaths should be taken only for serious matters. A false oath is calling on God as a witness to affirm a lie. The sin of perjury is making a promise under oath but then not keeping it. Both false oaths and perjury are abuses of God's name.

331 Our Christian name

In Baptism the Christian receives his or her name. This can be the name of a saint (who will be a model and make intercession for us) or a Christian mystery or virtue. Everyone's name is sacred and demands respect as a sign of the dignity of the one who bears it.

332 Calling on the name of God

Christians begin their day, their prayers, and
their activities with the sign of the cross.
Every morning we should dedicate the day
to the glory of God, calling on the name of
the Father and of the Son and of the Holy
Spirit. The sign of the cross strengthens us
against temptations and difficulties.

The Third Commandment

Remember the sabbath day, to keep it holy.
(Exodus 20: 8–10)

333 The Sabbath

The Sabbath is for the Lord, a day of rest, set
apart for the praise of God, his work of
creation, and his liberation of Israel from
Egypt. Sunday is the Christian Sabbath
because the Resurrection is the beginning of
the new creation, our true liberation and our
eternal rest in God.

334 The Lord's Day

The Lord's Day is a time for worship, rest
and doing works of mercy. Family needs or
important social service can legitimately
excuse us from the obligation of Sunday rest,
but all employers should avoid making

demands that hinder observing the Lord's Day.

335 Holy Days of Obligation

The Holy Days of Obligation normally include: the Nativity, Epiphany, the Ascension, the Body and Blood of Christ, Mary the Mother of God, the Immaculate Conception, the Assumption, and the feasts of Saint Joseph, the apostles Peter and Paul, and All Saints.

336 The Eucharist

Participation in the communal celebration of the Sunday Eucharist is a testimony to being faithful to Christ and to his Church. The faithful give witness to their unity of faith and charity, to God's holiness and their hope of salvation. Those who deliberately fail in this obligation commit a serious sin.

The Fourth Commandment

Honour your father and your mother. (Exodus 20: 12)

337 Honouring our father and mother

After God we should honour our parents to whom we owe life and the knowledge of

God. Children owe their parents respect, gratitude, just obedience, and assistance. The fourth commandment also requires that honour, affection, and gratitude be shown toward elders and ancestors.

338 Respect for all authority
We are obliged to honour, respect and fulfil our duties toward all whom God, for our good, has vested with his authority: instructors, teachers, leaders, magistrates, and others who govern. This commandment includes and presupposes the duties of those vested with authority.

339 The promised reward
If we observe this commandment we are promised a reward, the temporal fruits of peace and prosperity. Conversely, failure to observe it brings great harm to communities and to individuals.

340 The family
The family was created for the good of the spouses and the procreation and education of children. Thus, a man and a woman united in marriage, together with their children, form a family where all persons are equal in

dignity although differing in roles. The Christian family also has a missionary task to evangelize and to care for the young, the old, the sick, the handicapped and the poor.

341 Honouring the family

The importance of the family for the life and well-being of society entails a particular responsibility for society to support and strengthen marriage and the family, especially by ensuring the right to establish a family and bring up children in keeping with the family's religious and moral convictions.

342 The duties of parents

Parents have the first responsibility for the education of their children in a home where tenderness, forgiveness, respect, loyalty, and service are the rule. Parents must train their children to master themselves, to pray and discover their vocation, to consider the spiritual dimension of life as the most important, and to avoid compromising and degrading influences.

343 Adult children

When children become adults they assume responsibility for their own lives. They should still ask and receive their parents' advice. Parents should not push their children into a choice of a particular profession or spouse, but rather advise their children wisely, particularly when they start a family.

344 Respect for children's vocations

Family ties are important but not absolute. Parents should respect God's call on their children's lives, and encourage them to follow it. Parents should welcome the Lord's call to a child to follow him in virginity in the consecrated life or in priestly ministry.

345 The duties of citizens

Our responsibility for the common good obliges us to work with civil authorities for building up society in a spirit of truth, justice, solidarity, and freedom. We must also pay taxes, vote, defend our country, obey the law and offer prayer and thanks for all who exercise authority, because they are representatives of God.

346 Responding to abuse of authority

Even under the oppression of a public authority, citizens should still not refuse to do what is demanded of them by the common good; but it is legitimate for them to voice just criticism and to defend citizens' rights against the abuse of authority within the limits of the natural law and the Gospel.

The Fifth Commandment
You shall not kill. (Exodus 20: 13)

347 Respect for human life
Human life is sacred. It belongs to God alone from its beginning until its end: no one can under any circumstance claim the personal right directly to destroy an innocent human being.

348 Wrong attitudes
The fifth commandment also prohibits anger, hatred and vengeance. Christ's disciples are to turn the other cheek and love their enemies.

349 Murder
Murder is seriously wrong. The law forbidding it is universally valid: it obliges everyone, always and everywhere. The murder of one's children, brother, sister, parents or spouse are especially serious crimes by reason of the natural bonds which they break.

350 Self-defence

One is bound to take more care of one's own life than of another's. It is legitimate to insist on respect for one's own right to life. It is not murder to defend one's life even if one is forced to deal a deathly blow. The use of unnecessary violence in self-defence is unlawful.

351 The legitimate defence of life

Defending life can be not only a right but also a solemn duty for those who are responsible for others. The defence of the common good requires that an unjust aggressor be made unable to cause harm. For this reason, those who hold legitimate authority may sanction the use of arms to repel aggressors.

352 Punishment

Legitimate authorities have the right and duty to inflict punishment proportionate to an offence in order to defend public order and protect people's safety. The primary aim of such punishment is to redress the offence, but it should also have the purpose of correcting the guilty party.

353 The death penalty

The death penalty is not outlawed by the Church. However, if it is possible to defend and protect people's safety using non-deadly means, authority should limit itself to such means. Today the state has other options which make execution practically unnecessary.

354 Indirect killing

Doing anything with the intention of *indirectly* bringing about a person's death is seriously wrong, as is exposing someone to mortal danger without serious reason, or refusing assistance to a person in mortal danger. Killing someone unintentionally is not murder, but it may still be a serious offence depending on the conditions.

355 Abortion

Human life must be respected and protected from the moment of conception, the first moment of existence. Abortion, willed either as an end or a means, is seriously wrong, and carries the penalty of excommunication by the very commission of the offence. Formal co-operation in an abortion is also seriously wrong.

356 Genetics

Medical advancement cannot justify any murder. It is immoral to produce human embryos intended for exploitation as disposable biological material. Genetic manipulation aimed at producing human beings selected according to sex or other predetermined qualities is contrary to the dignity of a person.

357 Euthanasia

Direct euthanasia, whatever its motives and means, is morally unacceptable. Discontinuing medical procedures that are burdensome, dangerous, extraordinary, or disproportionate to the expected outcome can be legitimate.

358 Medical care

Sick or handicapped persons deserve special respect and should be helped to lead lives as normal as possible. Even if death is near, the ordinary care owed to the ill must be given. Painkillers that may hasten death can be used to alleviate the sufferings of the dying, if hastening death is not the intention.

359 Suicide

Suicide is a serious offence against God because our life belongs to him. We are its stewards, not its owners. Suicide also offends our neighbour because it unjustly breaks solidarity with those to whom we have obligations. It is also extremely contrary to the just love of self.

360 Suicide and salvation

Serious psychological problems or intense fear of suffering can diminish the responsibility of the one committing suicide. We should not despair of the salvation of those who have taken their own lives. By ways known to him alone, God can provide the opportunity for repentance.

361 The sin of scandal

Scandal is the sin of using one's power or position to lead others to do wrong. We are responsible for any evil we directly or indirectly encourage, because we become our neighbour's tempter. The sin of scandal involves anything leading to the decline of morals and the corruption of religious practice.

362 Respecting our health

The fifth commandment prohibits every kind of excess: the abuse of food, alcohol, tobacco, medicine and such like. The use of drugs, except on strictly therapeutic grounds, is seriously wrong. Wrongful producing of and trafficking in drugs are sins of scandal.

363 Science must respect moral criteria

Science and technology must respect fundamental moral criteria. They must be at the service of the individuals involved, respecting their rights, and true good. If they expose a person's life or psychological integrity to excessive risks they are illegitimate.

364 Respect for the dead

The dying should be given attention and care to help them live their last moments in dignity and peace. When they have died, their bodies must be treated with respect and in ways that reflect hope in the resurrection. This does not exclude autopsies conducted for legal inquests or scientific research.

365 Other sins against this commandment

Terrorism, kidnapping, hostage taking, torture, and mutilation are also morally wrong. The desire to do serious harm to someone is a serious sin. Even seeking vengeance toward someone who should be punished, is illicit.

366 The just war

Governments have the right of lawful self-defence when all the following are true:

- in order to avoid lasting, serious, and certain damage;
- where peaceful means are impractical or ineffective;
- where success will likely result; and
- where the arms used won't produce evils more serious than the evil to be eliminated.

367 Moral conduct during war

The moral law remains valid during armed conflict. Therefore:

- non-combatants, the wounded, and prisoners must be treated humanely;
- the extermination of a people, nation, or ethnic minority is a mortal sin; and
- any act of war directed to the destruction of whole cities is condemned.

The Sixth Commandment
You shall not commit adultery. (Exodus 20: 14)

368 The vocation to chastity
Jesus came to restore creation to the purity of its origins, therefore all baptized persons are called to lead chaste lives; that is, lives of sexual purity; according to their particular state of life. Chastity is self-mastery over one's desires and is a form of human freedom.

369 Offences against chastity: lust
Lust is a disordered desire for, or immoderate enjoyment of sexual pleasure. Sexual pleasure is morally disordered when sought for itself and isolated from its two primary purposes: procreation and unity in marriage.

370 Masturbation
Masturbation is the deliberate stimulation of the genital organs in order to derive sexual pleasure. It is, of itself, a seriously disordered action. Various psychological or social factors may lessen, or even minimize, moral culpability for this sin.

371 Fornication

Fornication is an act of sexual union between an unmarried man and an unmarried woman. It is seriously contrary to the natural order and to the dignity of persons and human sexuality. Moreover, it is a serious scandal when it involves corruption of the young.

372 Pornography

Pornography removes sexual acts from the intimacy of the partners, in order to display them deliberately to third parties. It degrades all its participants (actors, vendors, the public) and is a serious offence. Civil authorities should prevent its production and distribution.

373 Prostitution

Engaging in prostitution is always a serious sin. It reduces the person who engages in it to an instrument of sexual pleasure. The one who pays also sins seriously against himself, defiling his body, the temple of the Holy Spirit.

374 Rape

Rape is the forcible, sexual violation of another person. It is unjust, uncharitable and always evil. Incest and the rape or sexual abuse of children by those responsible for their education is especially serious.

375 Homosexual activity

Homosexual acts are, in themselves, always wrong. They are contrary to the natural law. They close the sexual act to the gift of life. They do not proceed from true affective and sexual complementarity.

376 Chastity and homosexuality

Homosexuals must be accepted with respect, compassion, and sensitivity. Unjust discrimination in their regard must be avoided. Homosexual persons are called to chastity. Like all Christians they should seek perfection by self-mastery, right friendships, prayer and sacramental grace.

377 The love of husband and wife

Sexual love, in which man and woman give themselves to one another, is proper and exclusive to spouses in marriage. Sexual acts are noble and honourable, and foster self-giving, joy and gratitude. The unity of the spouses fostered by sexual love is one of the purposes of marriage.

378 Marriage and procreation

The second purpose of sexual love is the transmission of life. Each and every marriage act must remain ordered *per se* to procreation. Married couples are thereby co-operating with the love of God the Creator.

379 Regulating having children

Spouses may seek to space the births of their children for just and unselfish reasons. Birth regulation based on the use of infertile periods is in conformity with the objective criteria of morality; however, any action which renders procreation impossible, whether before, during or after the sexual act, is wrong.

380 Infertility

Each child has a right to be born of a father and mother bound to each other by marriage. Therefore fertilization techniques that entail the intrusion of a person other than the couple (donation of sperm or ovum, surrogate uterus) are seriously immoral.

381 Sins against marriage

Adultery, divorce, polygamy, incest, trial marriage, and free union are serious offences against the dignity of marriage. The sexual act must take place exclusively within marriage. Outside of marriage it always constitutes a serious sin and excludes one from Holy Communion.

382 Adultery
Adultery consists in sexual relations between two persons, one or both of whom is married to someone else. Adulterers fail in their commitment, injure the sign of the covenant that marriage represents transgress the rights of the other spouse, and undermine the institution of marriage.

383 Divorce
Divorce is immoral because:
- it offends the covenant of salvation, of which sacramental marriage is a sign;
- it introduces disorder into the family and into society; and
- it brings significant harm to the deserted spouse and children.

The Seventh Commandment
You shall not steal. (Exodus 20: 15)

384 Handling earthly goods

The seventh commandment forbids unjustly taking or keeping anyone else's goods and requires the restitution of stolen goods to their owner. It commands justice and charity in the care of earthly goods, including caring for the common good of future humanity.

385 Private property

Private ownership of property supports the freedom and dignity of persons. It helps them to meet their basic needs and the needs of those in their charge. This right does not do away with the original gift of all the earth to the whole of the human race.

386 Caring for others

We should seek to use the goods we own not merely for ourselves but for the benefit of others as well. Those who hold many goods should use them with moderation, reserving the better part for guests, the sick and the poor.

387 Things we must not do

The seventh commandment forbids theft, keeping or wilfully damaging other's property, business fraud, paying unjust wages, pushing up prices unjustly, use of common goods for private purposes, work poorly done, tax evasion, forgery, excessive expenses, waste, and anything that leads to the enslavement of human beings.

388 Games of chance

Games of chance (card games, etc.) or wagers are not in themselves contrary to justice. They become morally unacceptable when they deprive someone of what is necessary or risk becoming an enslavement. Unfair wagers and cheating at games can constitute a serious matter.

389 Caring for animals

Because animals are God's creatures, we owe them kindness. It is contrary to human dignity to cause animals to suffer or die needlessly, but it is also unworthy to spend money on them that should as a priority go to the relief of human misery. It is legitimate to use animals for food and clothing.

390 Economic and social matters

The Church makes a moral judgement about economic and social matters, when the basic rights of the person or the salvation of souls requires it. The Church's social teaching proposes principles for reflection; it provides criteria for judgement; it gives guidelines for action.

391 The social doctrine of the Church
The Church teaches:

- Businesses are responsible for the economic and ecological effects of their operations.
- Social relationships must not be determined simply by economic factors.
- Profit is not an exclusive norm or ultimate end of economic activity.
- The basic rights of individuals and groups must always be respected.
- Work should be available to all to provide for themselves and their family.
- Access to employment and professions must be open to all without unjust discrimination.
- A strike is morally legitimate when it is necessary to obtain a proportionate benefit.
- We should use our talents to contribute to the benefit of all.

392 Work

We are called by God to prolong the work of creation by subduing the earth, both with and for one another. Hence work is a duty. Work honours the Creator's gifts and the talents received from him. Work can also be a means of sanctification. Work is for man, not man for work.

393 The state

The state must work to guarantee a stable currency and efficient public services, take concern for unemployment, and oversee and direct the exercise of human rights in the economic sector. Reasonable regulation of the marketplace for the common good is commended.

394 Justice among nations

Rich nations have a duty in solidarity and charity toward poor nations, especially in response to natural catastrophes. They must also support the efforts of poor countries working for growth and liberation. These tasks are specifically a part of the vocation of the lay faithful as citizens.

395 Immigration

More prosperous nations are obliged, to the extent they are able, to welcome immigrants. For the sake of the common good of their country, political authorities may make immigration subject to various conditions.

396 Love for the poor

God blesses those who come to the aid of the poor and rebukes those who turn away from them. Love for the poor extends not only to material poverty but also to the many forms of cultural and religious poverty. When we attend to the needs of those in want, we give them what is theirs, not ours.

397 The works of mercy

The spiritual works of mercy are instructing, advising, consoling, comforting, forgiving and bearing wrongs patiently. The corporal works of mercy are feeding the hungry, sheltering the homeless, clothing the naked, visiting the sick and imprisoned, and burying the dead, and especially giving alms to the poor.

The Eighth Commandment

You shall not bear false witness against your neighbour. (Exodus 20: 16)

398 What is forbidden, what is enjoined

The eighth commandment forbids misrepresenting the truth in ways such as lying, false witness, trickery, using a false pretence, and hypocrisy. These are unfaithfulness toward God, since God is truth. This commandment enjoins moral uprightness and so it forbids rash judgement, detraction, calumny, boasting, and using flattery to encourage another in wrong acts.

399 Witnessing to the truth of the Gospel

Witnessing to the Gospel is a duty for all Christians. It is an act of justice because it establishes the truth or makes it known. Martyrdom is the supreme witness given to the truth of the faith because it is bearing witness even unto death.

400 The purpose of speech

The purpose of speech is to communicate known truth to others. Deception is destructive of society. It undermines trust by violating truth and love. People cannot live with one another without mutual confidence that they are being truthful to one another.

401 Lying

The gravity of a lie is measured against: the nature of the truth it deforms, the circumstances, the intentions of the one who lies, and the harm suffered by its victims. Lying entails the duty of reparation.

402 Truthfulness

Truthfulness means taking concern for both honesty and discretion, for what ought to be expressed and what ought to be kept secret. Reasons for being silent or discreet include: the good and safety or privacy of others, and respect for the common good. No one is bound to reveal the truth to someone who does not have the right to know it.

403 The mass media

The media must not infringe upon an individual's privacy or freedom. The media must uphold the moral law, and the legitimate rights and dignity of every person. It must ensure that the information it communicates is true and – within the limits set by justice and charity – complete.

404 Using the mass media

Users of the mass media should practise

moderation and discipline in their approach. The mass media can give rise to passivity among users, making them less than vigilant about the morality and helpfulness of what is said or shown.

405 Truth and beauty

Truth is beautiful in itself. Human beings express the truth in a distinctively human form by using words. Artistry, in words and other forms of expression, reveals both beauty and truth. When inspired by love especially, art reflects the goodness of God and reveals the artist as a Creator in the likeness of God.

406 Sacred art

Sacred art has a particular vocation: evoking and glorifying the transcendent mystery of God. Genuine sacred art draws us to adoration, to prayer, and to the love of God as Creator, Saviour and Sanctifier. For this reason bishops should see to the promotion of good sacred art.

The Ninth Commandment

You shall not covet your neighbour's wife. (Exodus 20: 17)

407 Desiring another person's spouse

The ninth commandment forbids lustful desires. The baptized must struggle against disordered desires and seek purity of heart especially in three areas: charity; sexual behaviour; and orthodoxy of faith. To gain purity of heart demands prayer, the disciplining of one's feelings, eyes and imagination, the purification of intention, and the exercise of modesty.

408 Modesty

Modesty is a form of self-control. It refuses to unveil what should remain hidden. It inspires one's choice of clothing, and protects decency. It also avoids unhealthy curiosity and guides how one looks at and behaves toward others. It strengthens us to resist the charm of fashion and other pressures from the world.

The Tenth Commandment

You shall not covet your neighbour's goods. (Exodus 20: 17)

409 Desiring another person's goods

The tenth commandment forbids *coveting* the goods of another as the root of theft, robbery, and fraud. It forbids greed for money, goods, and power. Thus forbidden are such things as the *desire* for a monopoly in the marketplace or lucrative legal battles.

410 Trusting in God not goods

The tenth commandment tells us we won't find security in the abundance of goods; instead we are to trust in the Father and so be free from anxiety about our lives. Jesus says that to be his disciple means to renounce all that we have and to prefer him to everything and everyone.

Part Four

Prayer

Christian Prayer

411 What is prayer?
Prayer is both a gift from God and the natural response to God's faithful initiative of love. Prayer is the habit of being in the presence of God and in loving communion with him. In prayer one raises one's mind and heart to God or requests good things from God.

412 Praying from the heart
The 'heart' is the centre of our being, the place of truth, of decision making, where we choose life or death. It is the place of encounter with God, where the Holy Spirit and ourselves dwell together; and the place from where prayer springs forth.

413 The use of the psalms

The psalms are the masterwork of prayer in the Old Testament. Prayed by and fulfilled in Christ, the psalms are an essential and permanent part of the prayer of the Church. They are suitable for all people in every condition and time.

414 Our model for prayer

The Son of God who became Son of the Virgin learned to pray from his family and the people in the synagogue. In his human prayer he shows humble and trusting commitment of his human will to the Father. In contemplating the prayer of the Son of Man, the children of men learn to pray to God the Father.

415 Prayer in the age of the Church

The Spirit forms the Church in the life of prayer, inspiring new expressions of the same basic forms of prayer. The forms of prayer handed on from the early Church and those revealed in the Scriptures remain normative for Christian prayer.

416 Prayers of blessing

Because God blesses us, we, in return, bless

the One who is the source of every blessing. Our prayer ascends in the Holy Spirit through Christ to the Father and implores the blessing of the Holy Spirit whose blessing descends through Christ from the Father.

417 Prayers of adoration

In adoration we humbly acknowledge that we are but creatures before our Creator. Adoration is homage given in respectful silence to, and in the presence of, the ever-greater God.

418 Prayers of petition

In prayers of petition we ask, beseech, plead, invoke, entreat, and cry out to God for the things we personally need. We also express our awareness that we are creatures who are not our own beginning, not the masters of adversity, not our own last end, but sinners in need of help.

419 Prayers of intercession

Intercession is a prayer made on behalf of others. It is made in tune with God's mercy, even to the point of praying for those who do us harm. Christian intercession participates in Christ's intercession, and is also an expression of the communion of saints.

420 Prayers of thanksgiving

Thanksgiving characterizes the prayer of the Church, especially in celebrating the Eucharist, where she gives thanks for the work of salvation. This and every other event or need can be a basis for thanksgiving.

421 Prayers of praise

Praise is the form of prayer which recognizes most immediately that God is God. It rises to God, lauds him, and gives him glory for his own sake, quite beyond what he does but simply because he is. Praise embraces the other forms of prayer and carries them toward him who is its source and goal.

422 Christian prayer is Trinitarian

Christian prayer is Trinitarian. It begins with the Sign of the Cross. We normally pray to the Father, through the Son and in the Holy Spirit, but prayer may be addressed to Jesus Christ as well. We can also call directly upon the Holy Spirit, especially at the beginning of an important action, and so we pray, 'Come, Holy Spirit.'

423 The wellsprings of prayer

The Holy Spirit teaches us how to pray when we frequent the wellsprings of:

- the Word of God, which the Church strongly exhorts us to read frequently;
- the Liturgy of the Church;
- spiritual writings; and
- faith, in the hope of seeing God's face and the love of his presence – that is, through the theological virtues.

424 Common ways to pray

Calling on the holy name of Jesus is the simplest way of praying. Another simple and common formulation of prayer is: 'Lord Jesus Christ, Son of God, have mercy on me a sinner.' The Church also honours prayer to the Sacred Heart of Jesus and recommends the Stations of the Cross.

425 Praying with Mary

Because of Mary's co-operation with the action of the Holy Spirit, the Church loves to pray with her. We magnify the great things the Lord has done and entrust our supplication and praise to the Mother of Jesus.

426 The Hail Mary: Part 1

It was God himself, through the angel Gabriel, who said *Hail Mary*. He proclaimed her to be *full of grace* because the Son of God came to dwell in her. Elizabeth declared Mary *blessed among women* because she recognized the *blessed fruit of* Mary's *womb, Jesus*.

427 The Hail Mary: Part 2

Holy Mary, Mother of God. It is because Mary is the Mother of God and our mother that we can entrust all our cares and petitions to her: she will *pray for us sinners, now*, in the 'today' of our lives. We also surrender *the hour of our death* to her care. May she be there as she was at her son's death on the cross.

428 Learning to pray

The Christian family is the first place of education in prayer. It is in the 'domestic church' that God's children learn to pray, learn *about* prayer, and also learn *to persevere in* prayer. For young children in particular, daily family prayer and catechesis in prayer is of critical importance.

429 Places for prayer

The most appropriate places for prayer are

personal or family oratories, monasteries, places of pilgrimage, and above all church, which is the proper place for liturgical prayer for the parish community and the privileged place for Eucharistic adoration.

430 The cycle of prayer

The Church proposes certain rhythms of praying. Some are daily, such as morning and evening prayer, grace before and after meals, and the Liturgy of the Hours. The cycle of the liturgical year including Sundays and the great feasts also provides basic rhythms of the Christian's life of prayer.

431 Expressions of prayer: praying aloud

Vocal prayer is an essential element of the Christian life, Jesus both did it and taught it and it is unique to human beings. It corresponds to our human nature. We are body and soul, and so we pray with our whole being. Vocal prayer is also the form of prayer most expressive of solidarity with fellow worshippers.

432 Expressions of prayer: meditation

Meditation engages our reason, emotion, imagination and desire, and focuses them on the mysteries of Christ. Meditation makes use of the Bible, particularly the Gospels, the Lectionary, the writings of the spiritual fathers, books on spirituality, icons, the rosary and reflection on creation, history and one's own life.

433 Expressions of prayer: contemplation

Contemplative prayer simply seeks union with God. It is a gaze of faith, fixed on Jesus, and a renunciation of self. It is a communion of love, or 'silent love'. One must make time for contemplative prayer, with the firm determination not to give up. Yet it is also a gift that can be accepted only in humility.

434 Prayer is a battle

Prayer is a battle against our fallen nature and against those who tempt us to turn away from union with God. We must also battle against false notions of prayer: that it is just empty words and rituals, or an escape from reality or a waste of time because it is 'unproductive', or something counter to reason and science.

435 Failure in prayer

In addition, we battle with what we experience as failure in prayer, constant distraction, sloth, lack of faith, periods of dryness, discouragement that we have not given all to the Lord. We also may be disappointed over not being heard, in which case the Gospel invites us to ask ourselves about the conformity of our prayer to the desire of the Spirit.

The Lord's Prayer

436 The most perfect prayer

The Lord's Prayer is the most perfect of prayers. It is rightly at the core of the three sacraments of Christian initiation. It is the summary of all the prayers in Scripture. In it we ask for all the things we can rightly desire and in the order that they should be desired.

437 Abba, 'Father!'

The first phrase of the Lord's Prayer is a blessing of adoration for God's fatherhood. Although God always transcends our understanding, he has revealed himself to us as our Father and we enter into the mystery of his fatherhood in this prayer.

438 'Our' Father

When we say 'our' Father, we recognize that we have become 'his' people and he is henceforth 'our' God. This 'our' also expresses the certitude of our hope that all his covenant promises of love apply to us in Christ, especially the ultimate promise: the new Jerusalem.

439 Our unity

If we pray the Our Father sincerely, we leave individualism behind. If we are to say it truthfully, division among Christians has to be overcome. The baptized cannot pray to 'our' Father without bringing before him all those for whom he gave his beloved Son. God's love has no bounds, neither should our prayer.

440 Who art in heaven

Heaven is God's dwelling place, but this biblical expression does not mean a particular 'space' but a way of being; it does not mean that God is distant, but majestic. Our Father is not 'elsewhere', rather he is here, now, especially close to the humble and contrite of heart, even while he transcends everything and everywhere.

441 Hallowed be thy name

The holiness of God is the inaccessible centre of his eternal mystery. It is his 'glory'. When we 'hallow' God's name we do not make it holy – only God makes holy – but we recognize and praise his name as holy. This prayer is also a call to holiness for us. As he is holy so should we be holy.

442 Thy kingdom come

Praying 'Thy kingdom come' commits the Church to her mission in this present world. Although the fullness of the kingdom lies ahead of us and will only be fulfilled in the heavenly banquet, it comes to us already through Christ's death and Resurrection and through the Eucharist.

443 Thy will be done ...

The will of God can be summarized as 'Love one another, even as I have loved you.' In asking that his will be done, we acknowledge we are incapable of doing this on our own. We ask our Father to unite us to his will so that we can both understand it and do it.

444 Give us this day our daily bread

This petition glorifies our Father by acknowledging how good he is. 'Give us this day' reveals the trust of children who look to their Father for everything, at all times. The Father who gives us life also gives us the nourishment life requires – 'our bread' – both material and spiritual.

445 And forgive us our trespasses ...

In this petition we recognize that we are sinners asking for forgiveness. However, if we refuse to forgive others, even our enemies, our hearts are closed to the Father's merciful love. God's love is indivisible. It cannot enter our hearts if we refuse to forgive those who trespass against us.

446 And lead us not into temptation

Lead us not into temptation means, 'do not allow us to be tempted or yield to temptation'. God tempts no one. He wants to set us free from evil. Trials, which are necessary for spiritual growth, are different from temptation, which can lead to sin and death.

447 But deliver us from evil

Evil here refers to a person, Satan, the Evil

One. In this petition we ask to be delivered from all evils caused by him, present, past, and future. Victory over the Evil One was won once for all, when Jesus gave himself up to death to give us his life, but our total deliverance will happen only at the second coming.

448 The final doxology

The final doxology proclaims, 'For the Kingdom, the power and the glory are yours, now and for ever', repeating the first three petitions: the glorification of the Father's name, the coming of his reign, and the power of his saving will. These prayers join us in worship to the liturgy of heaven.

449 Amen!

After the prayer is over we say 'amen', which means 'so be it', thus ratifying what is contained in the prayer that God has taught us.

Notes

1   All notes refer to the paragraph numbers in the English edition of the *Catechism of the Catholic Church*, Geoffrey Chapman, London. This first is taken from paragraphs 27, 1718–1719, 1721.

2   CCC§30
3   CCC§31–33
4   CCC§37
5   CCC§40, 42
6   CCC§50, 54–64
7   CCC§65
8   CCC§77, 96
9   CCC§78, 83
10 CCC§85, 86
11 CCC§97, 129
12 CCC§105, 136, 107
13 CCC§109–111
14 CCC§120, 134
15 CCC§186, 194
16 CCC§176–177, 178
17 CCC§144, 148
18 CCC§150, 157, 180
19 CCC§153, 179, 161
20 CCC§162, 164
21 CCC§181
22 CCC§202
23 CCC§206, 213
24 CCC§209
25 CCC§216, 221
26 CCC§234
27 CCC§266
28 CCC§254, 267
29 CCC§239
30 CCC§269, 272
31 CCC§292
32 CCC§302
33 CCC§306–307
34 CCC§311
35 CCC§317–320
36 CCC§329–330
37 CCC§335–336
38 CCC§339–340
39 CCC§355–356
40 CCC§364, 366

41 CCC§369–372, 2333
42 CCC§370
43 CCC§374, 377
44 CCC§391–392
45 CCC§395
46 CCC§392, 397–398
47 CCC§399–400
48 CCC§405, 416–418
49 CCC§410–411, 421
50 CCC§430
51 CCC§436, 453
52 CCC§444–445
53 CCC§449–450
54 CCC§423, 461
55 CCC§457–460
56 CCC§464, 467
57 CCC§467, 470
58 CCC§485
59 CCC§499
60 CCC§467–468, 495
61 CCC§490–491
62 CCC§516, 520, 521
63 CCC§524
64 CCC§525, 526
65 CCC§528
66 CCC§504, 539, 612
67 CCC§597–598
68 CCC§601
69 CCC§613, 616
70 CCC§615
71 CCC§624, 630
72 CCC§632–633
73 CCC§638–639
74 CCC§645
75 CCC§648
76 CCC§651, 654
77 CCC§662, 665
78 CCC§663
79 CCC§673, 681, 954, 1040

[80] CCC§675
[81] CCC§682
[82] CCC§685, 264
[83] CCC§688
[84] CCC§692
[85] CCC§694
[86] CCC§695
[87] CCC§696–701
[88] CCC§708–718
[89] CCC§721, 725
[90] CCC§731, 732
[91] CCC§733–735
[92] CCC§751, 752
[93] CCC§764, 766
[94] CCC§765, 553
[95] CCC§770–771
[96] CCC§772–773
[97] CCC§774, 776
[98] CCC§782
[99] CCC§789, 806–807
[100] CCC§797
[101] CCC§811
[102] CCC§815, 866
[103] CCC§816
[104] CCC§817–818
[105] CCC§819
[106] CCC§822
[107] CCC§823–825
[108] CCC§828
[109] CCC§830–831
[110] CCC§837–838
[111] CCC§839
[112] CCC§841
[113] CCC§843
[114] CCC§846–847
[115] CCC§848–849
[116] CCC§857
[117] CCC§882
[118] CCC§883–885, 887
[119] CCC§889–891
[120] CCC§886, 892, 894
[121] CCC§893, 939
[122] CCC§898–899
[123] CCC§900
[124] CCC§901–903
[125] CCC§904–907
[126] CCC§908–909, 911
[127] CCC§932, 944
[128] CCC§950–953, 960
[129] CCC§948, 962
[130] CCC§956, 958
[131] CCC§967–970
[132] CCC§971
[133] CCC§966, 974
[134] CCC§977–978
[135] CCC§986, 982
[136] CCC§1008, 1013
[137] CCC§1015–1016
[138] CCC§1010
[139] CCC§1014
[140] CCC§1022
[141] CCC§1023, 1024, 1028
[142] CCC§1030–1031
[143] CCC§1033, 1037, 1057
[144] CCC§1038–1040
[145] CCC§1042–1043
[146] CCC§1061–1062, 1064
[147] CCC§1069–1070
[148] CCC§1082
[149] CCC§1081–1082
[150] CCC§1085
[151] CCC§1088
[152] CCC§1108, 1112
[153] CCC§1084, 1087, 1123
[154] CCC§1091
[155] CCC§1113
[156] CCC§1120, 1140
[157] CCC§1124–1125
[158] CCC§1127–1128
[159] CCC§1129
[160] CCC§1138–1139
[161] CCC§1146
[162] CCC§1145–1150
[163] CCC§1154
[164] CCC§1157
[165] CCC§1192
[166] CCC§1166, 1193
[167] CCC§1194
[168] CCC§1169, 1171
[169] CCC§1195
[170] CCC§1175, 1196
[171] CCC§1179
[172] CCC§1181–1186
[173] CCC§1200–1203
[174] CCC§1212
[175] CCC§1213

[176] CCC§1214
[177] CCC§1217–1222
[178] CCC§1229
[179] CCC§1235–1237
[180] CCC§1239–1243
[181] CCC§1247–1248
[182] CCC§1250
[183] CCC§1253–1254
[184] CCC§1253, 1255
[185] CCC§1256
[186] CCC§1257
[187] CCC§1263–1264
[188] CCC§1265–1266
[189] CCC§1267–1269
[190] CCC§1285
[191] CCC§1287–1288
[192] CCC§1295–1296, 1317
[193] CCC§1298, 1300
[194] CCC§1303
[195] CCC§1306, 1319
[196] CCC§1323
[197] CCC§1324, 1335
[198] CCC§1328–1332
[199] CCC§1333–1334
[200] CCC§1346
[201] CCC§1359, 1361
[202] CCC§1362–1366
[203] CCC§1368
[204] CCC§1373–1376
[205] CCC§1378
[206] CCC§1385, 1387
[207] CCC§1407, 1410–1411
[208] CCC§1389
[209] CCC§1391–1393
[210] CCC§1396
[211] CCC§1399
[212] CCC§1400
[213] CCC§1421
[214] CCC§1423–1424
[215] CCC§1421, 1426, 1432
[216] CCC§1444–1445
[217] CCC§1457–1458
[218] CCC§1448
[219] CCC§1480, 1483
[220] CCC§1450–1451, 1454
[221] CCC§1455–1456
[222] CCC§1461, 1466–1467
[223] CCC§1459–1460
[224] CCC§1434, 1438
[225] CCC§1468–1469, 1496
[226] CCC§1471–1472
[227] CCC§1506, 1510
[228] CCC§1517–1519
[229] CCC§1527–1529
[230] CCC§1524–1525
[231] CCC§1532
[232] CCC§1537–1538
[233] CCC§1546–1547
[234] CCC§1536, 874, 877
[235] CCC§1548–1550
[236] CCC§1555–1558
[237] CCC§1592, 1595
[238] CCC§1570, 1596
[239] CCC§1592, 1597
[240] CCC§1577–1578
[241] CCC§1579
[242] CCC§1618
[243] CCC§1603–1604, 1664
[244] CCC§1613, 1660
[245] CCC§1621
[246] CCC§1623, 1626–1628
[247] CCC§1660, 1629, 1664–1665
[248] CCC§1635–1636
[249] CCC§1641, 1661
[250] CCC§2361–2362, 1643
[251] CCC§1650–1651
[252] CCC§1656
[253] CCC§1658
[254] CCC§1667–1671
[255] CCC§1671–1672
[256] CCC§1673
[257] CCC§1674–1676
[258] CCC§1682
[259] CCC§1687–1690
[260] CCC§1717, 1726
[261] CCC§1700, 1704, 1730
[262] CCC§1704, 1706, 1707
[263] CCC§1734–1736
[264] CCC§1749–1752, 1754
[265] CCC§1753–1754
[266] CCC§1767–1768
[267] CCC§1776–1778
[268] CCC§1783–1785
[269] CCC§1791–1792
[270] CCC§1804, 1810

271 CCC§1806
272 CCC§1807
273 CCC§1808
274 CCC§1809
275 CCC§1812–1815
276 CCC§1817–1818, 1821
277 CCC§1822–1825, 1829
278 CCC§1826–1828
279 CCC§1830–1831
280 CCC§1832
281 CCC§1849–1850
282 CCC§1853
283 CCC§1866
284 CCC§1854–1855, 1857
285 CCC§1858, 1860
286 CCC§1856, 1861
287 CCC§1862–1863
288 CCC§1865
289 CCC§1868
290 CCC§1869
291 CCC§1879–1882
292 CCC§1883
293 CCC§1886, 1888
294 CCC§1898, 1901
295 CCC§1902, 1921
296 CCC§1906–1909
297 CCC§1934–1935
298 CCC§1940, 1948
299 CCC§1950, 1953
300 CCC§1952
301 CCC§1954–1955
302 CCC§1955–1959
303 CCC§1962–1963
304 CCC§1965–1966, 1971
305 CCC§1972
306 CCC§1987, 1993, 1999
307 CCC§1988–1991
308 CCC§2008, 2010
309 CCC§2013–2014
310 CCC§2041–2043
311 CCC§2044, 2062
312 CCC§2003–2004
313 CCC§2060–2062
314 CCC§2053, 2068, 2076
315 CCC§2069, 2072
316 CCC§2084, 2086
317 CCC§2086–2088
318 CCC§2087–2089
319 CCC§2090–2092
320 CCC§2093–2094
321 CCC§2096–2098
322 CCC§2101–2103
323 CCC§2112–2113
324 CCC§2132
325 CCC§2116–2117
326 CCC§2118–2121
327 CCC§2124–2125
328 CCC§2127–2128
329 CCC§2142, 2146, 2148
330 CCC§2149, 2152, 2155
331 CCC§2156
332 CCC§2157
333 CCC§2171, 2174, 2175
334 CCC§2185–2187
335 CCC§2177
336 CCC§2181–2182
337 CCC§2197, 2199, 2251
338 CCC§2199
339 CCC§2200
340 CCC§2201–2208
341 CCC§2210–2211
342 CCC§2223–2224, 2226
343 CCC§2230
344 CCC§2232–2233
345 CCC§2238–2240
346 CCC§2238, 2242
347 CCC§2258
348 CCC§2262
349 CCC§2261, 2268
350 CCC§2264
351 CCC§2265–2266
352 CCC§2266
353 CCC§2267
354 CCC§2269
355 CCC§2270–2272
356 CCC§2268, 2275
357 CCC§2277–2278
358 CCC§2279
359 CCC§2280–2281
360 CCC§2282–2283
361 CCC§2284–2287
362 CCC§2290–2291
363 CCC§2294–2296
364 CCC§2299–2301
365 CCC§2297, 2302
366 CCC§2308–2309

367 CCC§2312–2314
368 CCC§2336, 2394, 2339
369 CCC§2351
370 CCC§2352
371 CCC§2353
372 CCC§2354
373 CCC§2355
374 CCC§2356, 2389
375 CCC§2357
376 CCC§2358–2359
377 CCC§2361–2362
378 CCC§2363, 2366–2367
379 CCC§2368–2370
380 CCC§2376
381 CCC§2400, 2388–2391
382 CCC§2380–2381
383 CCC§2384–2385
384 CCC§2401, 2412, 2415
385 CCC§2402–2403
386 CCC§2404–2405
387 CCC§2408–2409, 2414
388 CCC§2413
389 CCC§2416–2418
390 CCC§2420, 2423
391 CCC§2423–2429, 2433, 2435
392 CCC§2427–2428
393 CCC§2431–2432, 2425
394 CCC§2439–2440, 2442
395 CCC§2241
396 CCC§2443–2444, 2446
397 CCC§2447
398 CCC§2464, 2468, 2476–2481
399 CCC§2472–2473
400 CCC§2485–2486
401 CCC§2484, 2487
402 CCC§2489
403 CCC§2492, 2494
404 CCC§2496
405 CCC§2500–2501
406 CCC§2502–2503
407 CCC§2514, 2518–2521
408 CCC§2521–2523
409 CCC§2534–2537
410 CCC§2544, 2547
411 CCC§2559, 2565, 2567
412 CCC§2563–2564
413 CCC§2596–2597
414 CCC§2599–2602
415 CCC§2623, 2625
416 CCC§2626–2627
417 CCC§2628
418 CCC§2629, 2646
419 CCC§2635
420 CCC§2637–2638
421 CCC§2639
422 CCC§2655, 2670–2671, 2166
423 CCC§2650–2658
424 CCC§2667–2669
425 CCC§2682
426 CCC§2676
427 CCC§2677
428 CCC§2685, 2688
429 CCC§2696
430 CCC§2698
431 CCC§2701–2702, 2704
432 CCC§2705, 2707–2708
433 CCC§2709–2717
434 CCC§2725–2727
435 CCC§2728–2733, 2756
436 CCC§2762–2763, 2768
437 CCC§2779, 2781
438 CCC§2787–2788
439 CCC§2792–2793
440 CCC§2794–2795
441 CCC§2807, 2809, 2813–2814
442 CCC§2816, 2818
443 CCC§2822, 2825–2826
444 CCC§2828, 2830
445 CCC§2839–2840, 2844
446 CCC§2846–2847
447 CCC§2851, 2853–2854
448 CCC§2855
449 CCC§2856